Healing Mercies

Standing on God's Promises

LUIS MEDINA

Trilogy Christian Publishers
A Wholly Owned Subsidiary of Trinity Broadcasting Network
2442 Michelle Drive
Tustin, CA 92780
Copyright © 2019 by Luis Medina

For information, address Trilogy Christian Publishing
Rights Department, 2442 Michelle Drive, Tustin, Ca 92780.
Trilogy Christian Publishing/ TBN and colophon are trademarks of Trinity Broadcasting Network.
For information about special discounts for bulk purchases, please contact Trilogy Christian Publishing.
Manufactured in the United States of America

10 9 8 7 6 5 4 3 2 1
Library of Congress Cataloging-in-Publication Data is available.
ISBN 978-1-64088-497-7
ISBN 978-1-64088-498-4

To my Heavenly Father,
Who promised never to leave me nor forsake me,
And delivered me from death.

Table of Contents

Introduction

On August 29th, 2017 in the emergency room, God gave me a life-changing testimony. The doctor's news that night flooded my heart with despair. Against overwhelming life-threatening conditions, I had to trust the unseen hand of God and His promises for me. God took a disease that had set its target on destroying me and killing my body, and exchanged it for a hope and a future. Today, I get to share how God touched me during my journey of faith for physical healing. I get to share how during this time, I experienced many tender moments filled with His presence, love, and joy. He began to heal my spirit man and do a new work in me.

We experienced countless moments of love as a family. My wife and sons refused to let my life go to waste. No matter how hard things got, they fought for me. My wife carried me. My sons lifted me up. My daughter-in-law encouraged me. They all went to battle with me and sometimes for me. I am better for knowing them. We witnessed moments of victory together. My extended family and family of believers, both near and far, played an important part in my healing and restoration.

Believe me when I say I'm no different than you. What God did for me, He can do for you. I experienced something I hadn't experienced before. I'm still overwhelmed by what happened. I think about it every day and constantly give thanks to God for waking me up yet another day. I'm thankful even for a single cup of water. (You'll see why.)

I'm writing this to share with you my testimony of God's faithfulness. I believe God has set this time for you to read this because you or somebody you know needs to hear it. They need to know they are not alone. If you are fighting for your life, you're going to have to surrender yourself and all that you are to God and trust in Him for your healing. My prayer is that during this season, you take hold of God's promises and apply them to your life. God has already done His part. I'm confident that as you do your part, He will exceed your expectations. Open wide your heart to receive God's love for you. Now is the day of salvation, and the accepted time of your testimony. Thanks for having me along your journey, in the name of Jesus, amen.

The End from the Beginning

God sees the end from the beginning every time, the things not yet seen or done in our lives. He is in the business of rebuilding and restoring that which is broken and broken down. His unseen hand is at work in our situation and in the midst of opposition. Nehemiah 2:18 reminds us, "Then I told them of the hand of my God which was good upon me." Nehemiah cried, fasted, prayed to God, and reminded God of His mercy. God answered his prayers, gave him favor with the king, provided protection, and made a way for the cupbearer to rebuild the walls of Jerusalem.

The God who used a cupbearer then is still the same God who rebuilds and restores broken bodies, hearts, relationships, families, marriages, faith, and more. There is no place one can hide, not even in the farthest horizon, that God cannot bring you back from and restore today. During my battle with end-stage liver cirrhosis, all I wanted was to be physically healed as quickly as possible. I just wanted the services God had to offer without taking the time to get to know Him. However, God had other plans for me. He did a work in me and healed me beyond just a physical healing.

Let me tell you about this God of Israel. He is the Father of Glory. He is holy and faithful. He is loving and caring. He loves the humble and shows mercy. He is the God of all comfort, who is able to comfort you in your suffering. He is the good, good Father like no earthly father will ever be. He sees our pain, hears our cries and prayers, and remembers His promises. He made a covenant for us through His Son, Jesus. It applies to everyone who confesses and repents of their sins and accepts Christ as their Lord and Savior. James 5:16 reminds us also to, "Confess your sins to each other and pray for each other so that you may be healed. The prayer of a righteous person is powerful and effective" (NIV). He will provide a way out for you in your situation.

When I was first diagnosed 16 months earlier and living with ascites, if you had told me that one day I would be standing and sharing my testimony before a congregation, I would not have believed it. Especially, when there appeared to be no end in sight to all the procedures I had to undergo. I had researched the condition many times over and trusted in doctors until I lost hope. In the middle of my valley, it was not easy to trust in God and let His hand go to work on my behalf. We tend to focus on our situation and make it bigger rather than focus on who God is and what His word can do for us.

After giving over 100 vials of blood and going through 35 paracentesis procedures, I was desperate and exhausted from carrying up to 19 extra pounds of water every week. This went on over a period of 16-months. I had to be drained on a weekly basis instead of every couple of weeks. I was in bondage and chained to the hospital. At times, I would be in the hospital for several hours as complications would arise. The procedures got so bad the nurses and technicians were having a difficult time getting my body to accept catheters. When they finally got a catheter in, they were not able to remove the water from my body. I was informed my peritoneum was scarred from all the paracentesis procedures. My body had reached its limits.

I kept trying to stir up my faith, but reality kept rearing its ugly head. The ongoing visits to the internal radiology department enforced restrictions on my lifestyle and my schedule and how far I could travel by car. Traveling by plane was not recommended due to the risks associated with my life-threatening condition. The doctors and specialists I had visited had no more explanations. The best medical term provided to describe my condition was "idiopathic cirrhosis" which technically means "having no origin or known cause." It was not alcohol related since I didn't drink. I had no more guarantees. I had reached my limit and began to cry out to God and pleaded with Him to heal me or take me home.

Jeremiah 29:11 reminds us, "For I know the plans I have for you," declares the Lord, "plans to prosper you and not to harm you, plans to give you hope and a future" (NIV). You may be chained to a hospital bed, or to your circumstances, but God's word cannot be chained. We know this to be truth. In 2 Timothy 2:9 we read, "For which I am suffering even to the point of being chained like a criminal. But God's word is not chained" (NIV). His word will accomplish His purpose and not return void. He is ready to forgive us, and to help us when we fail or fall and can no longer carry ourselves. Your suffering is not for nothing. Your circumstance did not catch God by surprise. God can use this time to deliver you, bring comfort in your suffering, to heal your soul (mind, will, and emotions), and more. No disease, substance, or life event is too great for the healing that God gives. He prepares our beds and restores us back from sickness. For by faith in Christ you stand.

There I was, on May 19th, 2019, standing before a congregation and sharing my testimony. As I stared into the audience, I could see how God used my valley to give hope to others, both in and out of the church. There are people hurting all around us. Whatever we are going through, we are being validated by God to be used to help others, to bless others as we are blessed—to spread the good news that Jesus still saves and heals. Embrace Him and His promises. Let God reveal His "hope and a future" for you as you seek Him. I'm glad that God wanted to reveal more for me than just a physical healing.

God's healing mercies cover spiritual healing, emotional healing, relational healing, and financial healing, as well. He is still restoring me every day into the person He wants me to be. I believe God is using my testimony to remind others of His love, salvation, forgiveness, faithfulness, mercy, grace, healing, restoration, and power for anyone going through a difficult situation. No sooner than I had finished giving my testimony, I felt led to pray for a man standing at the altar. At first, I hesitated, but felt the moment was slipping away so I went up and asked him if I could pray for a specific need.

To my surprise, he asked me to pray because he had received bad news concerning his health and was struggling with fear. I was shocked to find out later that day from his wife that he had told her how he wanted me to pray for him. Even when I hesitated, God's timing is impeccable. The man said he opened his eyes and I was standing before him. God factored in my initial hesitation and still worked it out. I thank God for the privilege of being able to pray for him. It was just as much for me as it was for him, as it built up my faith when I least expected it.

Dark Valley

You can expect at some point in your life you will experience a setback that will shake you to your core. It may be something that happens directly to you, to one of your family members, to a loved one, or to a close friend. When it happens, you'll find yourself standing at the entrance of your dark valley. Most of us would rather go around it and take the path of least resistance than to go through it and trust God, but often the path that requires faith is the path that leads to God and His eternal promises. You may wonder how you ended up in the valley. You may question yourself, or question God. For me, the decision was to either accept the medical report from the doctors as my final outcome or put my trust in God and my faith in Him for my healing.

To walk through my dark valley meant that I had to learn more about who God is, what He does, and how His word and promises apply to me in my situation. I had to put aside past religious experiences, new age beliefs, and my pride. It was time to get real with God and learn to be obedient to Him. I was no longer looking to use Him for what He could give me, but instead I was interested in a relationship with Him. In my valley, I learned that God is the same yesterday, today, and forever, and that there are hundreds of promises in the Bible that apply to me and my family. Armed with this knowledge of God's promises, I set out to beat this disease in the name of Jesus, amen. This was no longer my testimony alone, but a family testimony.

The surprising thing about this disease is you may be sick for decades and not even know it. It doesn't matter how old you are, if you eat a healthy diet, or exercise on a regular basis like I did, some diseases, such as liver cirrhosis, can take up to 10 years before they emerge. By the time you begin to experience some of the symptoms, the disease has already begun to wreak havoc in your body. One day you are feeling well and the next day you are suddenly diagnosed with a life-threatening condition, and your world is turned upside down. This is what happened to me.

Who you are, what you do for a living, or how much you earn doesn't really matter when a disease manifests itself. Your name and fame may buy you favor here but not in Heaven. Heaven operates on the currency of faith. Getting by and being a "good enough person" is simply just not enough to pull you through your dark valley. Money may buy you more time and excuses here, but it will not buy you salvation. And the worldly things you may seek here are of no eternal lasting value. What you do in your dark valley with your God-given gift of faith, and the choices you make, is all that matters.

I've heard it said that disease is not just a physical problem but rather a spiritual one. A condition that requires faith to fight and overcome it. My journey of faith may have started in a dark valley, but it didn't end there.

I Choose Life

This disease was designed to destroy me quickly and kill my body slowly. Although I was stricken with it and it unexpectedly left me in a downward spiral, I chose life over death, health over sickness, hope over hopelessness, and a new future over a predicable past. Inasmuch as I had become afflicted by this disease physically, I refused to be struck down by it. The more I listened to God's word, the more I could see areas of my life being transformed.

Today, I am a better Christian, husband, father, father-in-law, son, brother, and friend because of God's healing mercies, and everything He has taught me through this dark valley. I have been given an opportunity to share with you my testimony and God's hope for you. My testimony began over a year ago when the on-call doctor discovered the stage four liver cirrhosis on the awful night of August 29th, 2017. That was the night my world came tumbling down and my life changed forever. The doctor working the emergency late shift at the hospital walked in my room and said, "You have end-stage liver cirrhosis." This is the news I got about two hours after checking in to the emergency room. My blood work revealed elevated liver enzymes and the CT scan showed my liver was very scarred and decompensated. My health had immediately taken a turn for the worse and there was nothing I could do but die a slow and painful death or get a transplant.

I was now deep in despair and seeking answers. The book of Mark 9:23 says "Everything is possible for one who believes" (NIV). I wish I could tell you that these words ran across my mind, or that I was a strong man of faith and un-afraid that night, but the truth is, I was neither. I was in shock and my body was weak. I was spiritually bankrupt and devoid of hope. At the time, I had no desire to know about God except to know why He would allow this to happen to me. I wasn't an alcohol drinker, I ate a clean diet, and I exercised six times per week. I didn't even smoke because it's bad for your health.

The events of that night happened so suddenly, and the whole situation was so surreal, I didn't know what to feel or how to react. I knew it was important to hold on and not to let my mind shut down since my body would follow next. I knew I had a lot of fight left in me and I wasn't ready to give up. One thing I learned is of all the organs in the body, the liver is the only one that can regenerate itself. The deteriorating condition of my liver had started decades ago and had gone undetect-ed by my previous doctors. According to the doctor, the scan showed extreme liver scarring to the point of no return. The doctor said that my liver appeared as if I had "been drinking vodka every day for the past 20 years." She insisted that I stay overnight to be seen by several specialists. When I declined to stay overnight but instead return in the morning, the doctor said emphatically, "liver failure is a terrible way to die...slow and painful."

The doctor failed to mention that having end-stage cirrhosis of the liver is also a terrible way to live! She didn't clue me in on the extreme lifestyle changes that would be required, including weekly paracentesis to drain up to 19lbs of fluid to alleviate pressure in my body. I was essentially tethered to the hospital radiology department and my personal plans revolved around being in the hospital every 5 to 7 days. She proceeded to ask me if I would like to speak with a priest or a pastor. My wife and I looked at each other in complete disbelief.

Later that night, my wife and I wept together in our hospital room. All of our plans, dreams, goals, and future were now on hold, indefinitely. To be honest, having been bombarded with all that bad news at once made it difficult for me to see beyond the night, let alone a brighter future ahead of us. The doctor's question of whether I wanted to speak with a pastor or priest that night lingered in my mind, but I did not consider seeing either of them. There was no pastor I could trust at the time. By all accounts, it seemed like my time was up and there was nothing I could do to turn back that hands of time or return to the way things used to be.

Sometimes due to unforeseen circumstances beyond our control, we fail to see the invisible. We lose heart and our confidence when we walk by sight and not by faith in God. We are tempted by the whispers of a serpent to reject, blame, and doubt God and His love for us. The pain God reveals is the pain God can heal, when we let Him. Therefore walk by faith day by day, knowing that your physical condition is temporary, and God's unseen hand is at work right now in your life.

Death Sentence

That night, the doctor didn't just deliver her diagnosis, she delivered a death sentence to my wife and I. The whole thing was sickening to us and didn't make any sense. I had just been at the gym and jogged several miles earlier in the week. To go from my normal routine at the gym and my usual healthy diet to being admitted in the hospital, we were just not prepared for the drastic change brought by this life-altering disease. I was in denial and didn't want to deal with what was happening to me and what was about to unfold next. This disease was an unwarranted intrusion and serious threat upon my life and our lifestyle. I couldn't understand how my health just plummeted overnight. I had fallen into a pit that I could not get out of and was in desperate need of help.

We were new in Atlanta, Georgia, and did not have a pastor or home church family at the time to call for prayer and spiritual support. Thank God that my oldest son, Matt, and his wife, Amanda, were living here and were able to visit and comfort us in the hospital early in the morning upon receiving our call. My youngest son, Gabe, was traveling at the time, but called the minute he got the news and was back in the United States. Notifying my two sons and the rest of the family were the toughest calls I had ever made. I thought I was going to die soon. I remember telling Matt to keep on singing no matter what happened to me. I was completely heartbroken. We wept on the phone. I feared not being able to finish what we had started together.

Why Me, God?

Who you think you are or how tough you think you are, isn't as important as how willing you are to be vulnerable and allow God to use you. His strength is demonstrated in our weakness. He will use you and your situation to teach you, correct you, and grow you beyond your physical health. That night as I laid in bed staring out the hospital window early into the morning, my wife asleep on the chair, I was trying to process everything that had just happened. I was completely overwhelmed and terrified at the thought of dying and facing God. I let a passion of mine, bodybuilding, consume all my time and it had become my idol.

I was obsessed with weight lifting and the natural high and confidence that came with it. It was the one thing I could control and didn't need to pray or wait on God to answer prayers or see instant growth in this area. I realize now that I had taken my eyes off God and focused them on myself instead. To make things worse, I was practicing the law of attraction and the physical manifestation of thoughts and energy. I began to worship God's creation and no longer the Creator. I had completely backslid from my faith and first love and had become a man destitute of God's love. I needed His forgiveness, mercy, grace—another chance.

I was taking God for granted and no longer spending time in the Word of God. I didn't allow God to lead and develop me through the finished work of Jesus Christ. Everything I need to live for God, He accomplished for me by His work in Christ. I allowed the lust of the flesh, the lust of the eyes, and the pride of life, instead of the power of the Cross, to rule over me. I was walking in the flesh, and in bondage to worldly influence. I had hardened my heart and could no longer hear Him.

What Did I Do to Deserve This?

I did not hear from God that night and if He was speaking, I was too emotionally numb to listen. I was sinking in quicksand, trying to get out with no lifeline. My faith was almost non-existent. I started to vent my frustration and blame God. I began asking questions like: "Why me, God? Why would you allow such a thing in my life? What is the purpose of this? Why now? What did I do to deserve this?" I accused God of planting a time-release grenade in my body when I was a young man that would explode in my face decades later. I felt abandoned and was slipping into depression and isolating behavior.

There were days when I wondered if I had used up all my second chances with God. I wasn't sure if practicing the law of attraction had also brought some of this on. I remember getting up every morning and reciting phrases like, "I am the receiver of great wealth" and "I am the receiver of great health." I believed it and would repeat these words of positive reinforcement over and over throughout the day. I even started to believe in luck and played several lottery scratch tickets and won thousands of dollars, which was enough to keep me going back for more.

I regret studying the law of attraction, new age beliefs, and spending over a year reading books and watching videos on the topic. Something just didn't feel right. I had changed and become someone more dependent on an unknown universal entity for good fortune than in a relationship with my Heavenly Father. It took the doctor's news and my dark valley for me to turn to God. That night, I needed something more tangible than just a positive energy attraction from the universe. I needed not only to confess and repent of my sins but to also do a 180-degree about-face and return to God. I was no longer willing to believe in the universe to provide something it cannot provide. I needed salvation and a personal relationship with my Lord God—My Elohim.

Two years prior to being diagnosed, I had started attending a local gym and began exercising at least two hours every day, six days a week, and sometimes more than that. I started to do a double session, one in the morning, and another at night. The results were incredible: I had achieved huge gains in muscle—including traps, shoulders, biceps, and back. I was on a roll and working on developing my chest, legs, and abs for an overall symmetrical build, as I prepared to enter amateur bodybuilding at age fifty.

Obsessed and Lost

I was so hooked on the gym and fitness lifestyle it became my drug and my high. The more I lifted weights and worked out the better I felt. I felt unstoppable and age to me was nothing more than a number. I packed on muscle left and right and maintained a weight of about 210 pounds. The gym became my outlet to escape the world and release stress.

My best memories at the gym are the times I got to play full court basketball with my sons for hours non-stop, some-times several times during the week. We joined the gym's adult basketball league and played a full season, which was fun. It was a great bonding experience with my sons which I will never forget. I was known for hitting the threes while my two sons would take care of business inside the paint, and just about anywhere from the three-point line.

My challenge at the time was trying to eat enough protein each day to maintain my muscle mass. I could not consume enough poultry or fish to reach my desired intake of at least 175 grams of protein a day. I would often use whey powder, egg whites, or plant-based protein shakes to supplement my daily protein intake. I preferred to get my protein from actual food rather than from powder. Soon after I started weight lifting, I wanted to encourage other people over forty to exercise and find the fun in working out. I launched an Instagram account to show my progress. The account gained thousands of followers over time from across the world, which further motivated me to keep going.

The gym staff noticed that I was there most of the time, and they would sometimes stop by to see what body part I was working on that day or night. I have to admit, having that kind of attention was pretty cool at first. I was on another level of working out and by this time bodybuilding had become my religion. It was my thing and I owned it! No one could tell me otherwise or take it away. What I did not realize then is that I was so deep into working out that I had lost my balance. Gym life had taken over every aspect of my personal life.

I became so obsessed with weightlifting that my attitude changed and then my priorities shifted. I let my competitive nature take over the better part of me as well. I considered everyone around me to be my competitor. I just had to be better than everyone in and out of the gym. I then made the decision to eat clean and switched from eating conventional foods to organic or non-genetically modified organisms (GMO) foods. I was feeling good, lighter, and less bloated. I began losing weight without any effort. I read an article about how much strain meat puts on the body and how much energy is required to digest it so I decided to become a vegetarian.

I immediately stopped eating meat and took it a step further and removed dairy and soy from my diet. In hindsight, changing my diet so drastically was probably not a wise move. I should have done more research before making such a major change to my body. Maybe things would be different today but there is no way to tell. I think I did more harm to my body than good by denying it the vitamin B12 one gets from meat. Doctors have told me that becoming a vegetarian and not getting enough B12 is the culprit to liver disease in my situation. I didn't buy it.

Since I had a lot of energy and felt good all the time, it never dawned on me that there was a potential health-related problem lurking in my body. In my mind, I was doing all the right things, being smart, and taking care of my health. If I got the flu, I would rather endure pain and fever than take a single aspirin or cough medicine, which is a good thing since both can hurt the liver. I am glad that I did not drink alcohol or wine since I later found out that both begin to kill liver cells the minute you drink either of them.

I remembered reading the scriptures when I was first saved in my twenties that our body is the temple of the Holy Spirit. 1 Corinthians 6:19 says, "Or do you not know that your body is the temple of the Holy Spirit who is in you, whom you have from God, and you are not your own." If my body is the temple then I am the guardian of it, and I will try not to consume any chemically altered food, drink liquor of any kind, or smoke.

A Deeper Purpose

When this awful disease struck, my dreams of becoming an amateur bodybuilder and fitness guru were no longer a part of my future. Soon after the illness manifested, I found out there was more to God's plans for my life than I had expected. In fact, today I don't want to go back to the gym as I'm a changed man. I prefer to lift concrete blocks in my backyard than to be at the gym. I'll only go with my wife or my sons twice a week. I don't know what stage of life you're in or what disease you may be going through, but there is a deeper purpose for you to discover in God. I had to go through my dark valley, and it stopped me dead on my tracks. I urge you to seek your calling with all your heart and not give up. You will find there is always someone worse off than you who can use your help and encouragement. Along your journey of faith, look for the timing of the Holy Spirit to lead you. Consider that as you bless others, you too will be blessed. There is something wonderful and powerful awaiting you when you open yourself up to God and allow Him to work in and through you, in the name of Jesus. He is on the mountain top and in the dark valley. He is for you and His presence goes with you. You are not alone.

Drawing Closer to God

God used this life-threatening situation to draw me closer to Him; to teach me about His Holy Spirit; to help me forgive others, including myself; to mend broken relationships and create new ones; to heal past hurts and bring closure to so many issues; to give me faith that endures; to set me free; and to seal my future with Him. I was delivered from so many life issues and brokenness. Some people can live a lifetime and not get healed or recover from so much while on Earth. I thank God for His healing mercies and that He has a perfect will for each of us. The promise of "everything is possible..." started to take root in my journey of faith.

The gastroenterologist stopped by my room to further explain the medical conditions surrounding stage-four cirrhosis. I was scheduled for my first paracentesis that same morning. (A paracentesis is a procedure to drain excessive bodily fluid in the abdomen cavity using a hollow needle. This is needed to alleviate ascites due to the liver's inability to metabolize protein, fat, and carbohydrates.) They removed over 14 lbs. of fluid. This procedure became very frequent with more than 35 procedures completed and hundreds of liters of fluid removed over the course of 16 months. I quickly became known as "a regular" at the hospital with the folks at the front desk and in the interventional radiology (IR) department, where I met some of the kindest people.

A couple of months after being released from the hospital, I went through a wide range of emotions, from anger to depression, and just wanted to be left alone. The doctor's version of my new reality was not good, and I did not want to accept it. I was a wreck and had hit the lowest point in my life. A cure could not come fast enough. I started to sever ties with all those around me, including my family. It wasn't anything anyone had done to me; I just could no longer feel any kind of hope or see a bright future. I would go into my room day and night and lay in bed and weep with this dark cloud over me. I cried at home, at work, in my car, in the stores, and just about everywhere I went. This coming from a guy who believed that men should not cry and any man who cried was weak. I wanted to move out and crawl into a small space somewhere and be left alone to die.

I remember walking with my wife, whom I have known for over 36 years, since I was a freshman in high school, and telling her that I did not want her to suffer with me and gave her a pass to divorce me. I did not want to be a burden to her or my two sons. I also told my oldest son, who had helped me overcome many challenges and become a better father. He was so upset that I would even consider such a thought and did not give up on me. My family was willing to go to battle with me, yet there were times when I wanted to retreat. I am so thankful to have such a wonderful and supportive family at my side.

During my valley, I believe God was revealing His love

and word to me, and used this time to draw me closer to Him through many scriptures. My favorite was from the book of Jeremiah 29, verse 11, "For I know the plans I have for you," declares the Lord, "plans to prosper you and not to harm you, plans to give you hope and a future" (NIV). God's word gave me life, a hope, and a future. When I thought it was over, God reminded me that He has the final say over my life.

I didn't know at the time that the liver performs hundreds of functions; such as filtering toxins, cleaning blood, and internalizing feelings, to name a few. I wondered how much of the latter (that is, internalizing feelings) had to do with the fast deterioration of my liver, given my rough experience growing up as a child. My first hepatologist was working me up to meet the transplant center at a hospital in Atlanta. He did not want to explore the option for my liver to regenerate. My Model for End-Stage Liver Disease (MELD) score of 16 did not qualify me to get on the waiting list for an organ transplant since it did not meet the minimum score of 18.

When my MELD score did go up to a score of 18, it then dropped to a score of 14 a month later. I did not expect a traditional hepatologist to endorse a complementary protocol based on alternative treatments, but I wanted to explore a natural or a combination of traditional and integrative options. I feel there is more to medical treatment than just the western practice of medicine. The medical report showed that my albumin level was too low, my bilirubin level was too high, and my sodium level was too low. The hepatologist told me there was nothing I could do to change these numbers, especially my bilirubin.

"No amount of exercise or diet could change these numbers," said the hepatologist. I remember saying to him, "I can pray," and he looked at me a certain way and tried to encourage me, but it didn't feel real. It was then that I decided to get a second opinion from a consultant who "practices alternative medicine." He quickly informed me that he was familiar with the hepatologist's credentials and added that the liver had been so scarred it was beyond regeneration. When I told the consultant the same thing I had told the hepatologist about how we can pray, he said "You better pray that your hepatologist is available when the time comes for your transplant." By now, I had met with a hepatologist, hematologist, gastroenterologist, an alternative medicine consultant, and several naturopathic doctors.

My wife and I left his office so overwhelmed by the negative news and the spirit of disbelief around us. We wept along the way and forgot where we had parked our car. It was cloudy and dark outside that afternoon and we felt lost and hopeless. Sure enough, that cloud of despair was there hovering over us again. Then it hit me! The doctors are reading the numbers from lab work, so in order to change their position and attitude, we have to pray to God for the numbers to improve and get within normal range. Maybe then the doctors would acknowledge that prayer works. If they chose not to acknowledge it, it's on them and they would have to live with that.

I understand that doctors cannot promote anything the FDA has not approved, and some doctors, not all, are more interested in what drugs big pharma pushes than finding the root cause of a disease, but a little display of compassion and less god-like complex would be nice. It would take a special kind of doctor to believe in medical science and have faith in God. By this time, I had lost about 50 pounds, including my facial muscles and so I didn't look anything like myself.

Crying Out to God

My face used to be filled in and I looked much younger before being diagnosed. I used to weigh about 210 lbs. and in a couple of months my weight plunged to a new low of 160 lbs. I could not eat enough to maintain my weight, much less put on weight. All my muscle gains from the previous two years were gone. I had to eat every 2-3 hours just to keep my body from crashing and deteriorating further. I could eat all the carbohydrates I wanted and still not gain any weight.

This was quite a difference from before. Eating felt more like work. Often times, after a paracentesis, I just wanted to go home and get some rest, but this was not always possible due to work. I had to adjust to the new reality of going to work while dealing with an ongoing medical condition and the procedures it required. There were days as the weather got cold, when my feet swelled up so badly they felt like blocks of ice and I could barely walk from the elevator to my car. I remember getting home one day in so much pain I cried out to God to heal me or give me relief. Soon after that I received relief.

Along with the disease came stares from people in the

workplace and in public. As my face began to lose more muscle tissue and my stomach started to grow with fluid, some people stared and were obvious while others were more discreet, but I could still see them from the corner of my eye. It is ironic, one day I'm working on getting six-pack abs and the next I'm dealing with ascites and looking pregnant.

The most uncomfortable feeling was when my reporting manager would just stare at my stomach while I was seated in my cubicle. Some days it affected me and other days I just didn't care. I had accepted my new physical appearance for the time. I began to wear all black clothes with a fleece jacket even in hot temperatures and at work since I could no longer hide the way I looked. All my efforts to do the right thing, including eating healthy and exercising regularly throughout most of my life didn't matter. Every decision thought to be good and promoted in our society had brought me to this new low in my life.

Taken for Granted

I often wondered if everyone at work had to go through the same thing, how long would it be before they stopped pretending, gave up, and quit. It seemed like every week there was an email about free food available in the kitchen. Sometimes my colleagues would bring company-sponsored lunches to me not knowing my medical condition. As much as I wanted to join them, I had to decline their offer. Per the doctor's order, I could not eat anything processed, fried, spicy, or that had gluten—all the foods I once had taken for granted when I was healthy and before becoming a vegetarian.

I had this intense craving for Pizza Hut's Pepperoni Lover's Pizza. Not only was this pizza a savory dish, but I had formed an emotional connection to it earlier in my youth, ever since my biological father treated me to this dish whenever he would visit. Every now and then, I would eat some fast food, but nothing more than the average person would eat, and not to mention, I exercised regularly a good part of my life.

As of today, the root cause of my medical condition is still unknown. The doctors and specialists cannot figure it out.

They use the term "idiopathic cirrhosis" but really that is just another way of saying, We do not understand the origin of your cirrhosis. We don't know for sure what the is the root cause of why you are the way you are.

Several professionals have given me their opinions on what brought on end-stage liver cirrhosis, ranging from being 20 lbs. overweight, to being a vegetarian, to consuming foods with high fructose corn syrup. Why then is not half of the population in the United States sick and experiencing this awful disease. Today, we have more overweight people, more vegetarians, and more people eating foods with high fructose corn syrup than ever before.

Facing My Giant

Over the next year I learned about all my conditions related to end-stage non-alcoholic liver cirrhosis, such as ascites, portal hypertension, thrombosis, varices, and splenomegaly (enlarged spleen), on top of being anemic. I spent a good part of the year in appointments with a hepatologist, hematologist, gastroenterologist, PCP, dietician; at the family clinic and integrative clinic; seeking both conventional and alternative treatments. I subjected my body to lab work (hundreds of vials), IV therapies, coffee enemas, acupuncture, bio electrotherapy, light therapy, paracentesis, and infrared saunas. Pretty much everything you can imagine under the sun, except prayer and to truly understand God's will and plan for me.

I was very vulnerable and requested prayer from everyone, including seeking the advice from others of different faiths and professionals in the holistic field. I almost purchased a healing saint candle before my son and daughter-in-law called me to remind me of my Christian faith. They knew I was a Christian and my faith was based on the New King James Version bible which did not support praying to saints, only to God, our Heavenly Father, in the name of Jesus Christ.

Why Blame God

I began thinking, *Why am I blaming God for this?* As far as I know, I could have been the one to sabotage my health and bring this on. I was used to doing that in other areas of my personal life. I had stiffed-armed and pushed away everybody who had ever tried to get close to me. Perhaps I deserved everything that was happening. Clearly, I was using the gym to masquerade some deeper, personal issues. For some of you to fully let go of all unforgiveness, it may require taking the step to forgive God for any resentment you may have had against Him, then forgive yourself and everyone else who has ever hurt you. Until you do this, you will not start with a clean slate.

Healing Mercies

My healing as a father occurred when Matt took the time to notice my on-going need to keep proving myself at the gym. After many late-night discussions, which sometimes would turn into arguments that would last for hours, he began to break down the many defensive barriers I had subconsciously developed growing up in the streets. This healing didn't just happen overnight. He and I would spar constantly as he tried to get closer to me about my frustration. I'll never forget the night the breakthrough happened. We were living in Georgia. Matt and I were standing in the kitchen one evening talking, when it became clear to me the reason why I was always trying to prove myself at work, in the gym, and in life, was because I didn't think I was good enough for my biological father's love and relationship. Matt was right and I was wrong.

Here I was at 48 years old, having lived most of my life always rejecting others and sabotaging my relationships to avoid being rejected. You would think that a man of my age could get over not having his dad present for most of his life and move on, but that was not the case with me. Not having my dad around meant I had no role model to help me raise my sons. The feeling of rejection can make a person do stupid things, like live a life in isolation and develop a judgmental mindset. I would often stiff-arm anyone trying to get close to me to avoid rejection. They say, "Hurting people hurt people," and I can attest to that.

Forgiving Others

It wasn't until Matt suggested I address my feelings with my dad that I was truly healed from past hurts and brought closure to my feelings of brokenness. I remembered calling my dad one afternoon and we both wept as I asked him to forgive me for not being a better son, and I also forgave him. We agreed that while we couldn't go back and change the past, we would build the best father and son relationship we could moving forward. In October of 2018, I was able to visit my dad and spend a few days together as father and son for the first time. It was awesome! I was not only healed as a father, but also as a son.

Forgiving Myself

My next healing came when I learned to forgive myself—
something that had never crossed my mind. Before you can
truly forgive others, you must learn to forgive yourself, just as
God has forgiven you. Only then are you able to forgive others. You can only give that which you have received. The book
of Ephesians 4:31-32 says, "Get rid of all bitterness, rage, and
anger, brawling and slander, along with every form of malice.
Be kind and compassionate to one another, forgiving each other, just as in Christ God forgave you" (NIV).

After forgiving myself, it became easier to forgive others. I started asking for forgiveness from both of my sons, my
wife, my daughter-in-law, my mom, my siblings, and anyone
the Holy Spirit would reveal to me. So much of healing is
connected to forgiveness and it's very important not to hold a
grudge or resentment towards anyone. I learned that forgiveness is really for you and not so much for the other person.
It's important to free yourself from holding on to unforgiveness—not only is unforgiveness unscriptural, but it is also
toxic to your mind, spirit, and body. Unforgiveness will delay

your healing. Emotions, such as anger and frustration, are also known to affect the liver.

Without the help of God and the family He blessed me with, I would not have been able to pull through with my life on the line. It took the support of my wife, sons, father, mother, daughter-in-law, and brothers to keep me from sinking further. I can't begin to tell you how much time in prayer to God my family put in for me, especially my son Matt and his wife, Amanda. How before and after each doctor's appointment, procedure, or negative report, they just kept pouring God's word into me, and reminded me that God is faithful. They continued to pour God's love and encouragement to my wife and I with every single visit, call, and text. My son, Gabe, was also there for me with encouragement, too. I still remember what he said to me at the outset of this situation, he said, "Dad I know you are going to go ham on this disease." It's amazing to know after my sons saw me in my weakest state and unable to carry myself out of bed, they still looked up to me. The night before my critical surgery, Gabe called and we wept just after he said, "Dad no matter what happens tomorrow, I just want you to know that I'm proud of you and wanted you to know it."

I can't imagine the emotional strain this whole situation has put on my sons and their loved ones. The questions Matt and Gabe must have had, the prayers to God, and the thoughts that God heard from both these young men. The thought of not knowing if their earthly father would be taken out this early in life had to weigh heavy on their hearts. I'm so blessed to have two amazing sons who have also taught me so much about how to be a better father.

My wife lived through this whole ordeal with me twenty-four hours a day. She literally did all the heavy lifting, both spiritually and physically, and never stopped loving and encouraging me. I could write an entire book just on everything she has done for me during the 16 months alone. Not only did we enter a new phase in life as empty nesters, but through this experience we have grown closer to each other and pray with more intensity than ever before.

Spiritual Attacks

As my health continued to deteriorate, my biological dad saw a picture of me with my brother, Dennis, visiting from Massachusetts on Facebook and was concerned about my health. About a month later, both he and my brother, Coquito, flew from Florida to check up on me. During this visit, I learned about my body being under "spiritual attack." My brother had become a pastor earlier in the year and moved to Kissimmee, Florida, to start a new church called Casa Paternal. He began to break down the spiritual side of things that were happening to me, and how it was illegal for sickness to attach itself to my body.

Doctors Can't Explain It

My brother began to open my eyes up to the existence of another realm, a spiritual battlefield, where we "wrestle not against flesh and blood but against principalities, powers, rulers of darkness, and spiritual wickedness." (See Ephesians 6:12.) He and his wife began lifting me up in prayer and reminding me of God's word on spiritual warfare. My brother also began declaring healing over me. The idea that I was under a spiritual attack wasn't farfetched and it certainly provided a fresh perspective on my situation.

By this time, my family and brothers-in-Christ, all around the United States, were lifting me up in prayer. Let me tell you, the timing of some of their calls or texts was so precise my wife and I were often astounded at how quickly God could bring a word of encouragement to us, just after we had heard another bad medical report.

At first, I gave no thought to any medical treatment, since I didn't consider anyone who received them miraculously healed. I wanted supernatural healing from God only. Yet, if I was to be healed, I would have to humble myself and completely turn over my situation and disease to God. I later found out that part of what was delaying my healing was my pride. I had to confess and repent of my pride and put my faith in God for my healing. I had to allow Him to heal me, His way and on His terms, and not my way or on my timetable. It didn't occur to me that the entire time, I was trying to tell God how to heal me and when to do the healing.

How could I have been so foolish to think I could twist God's arm to bend to my will. Until you are ready to completely give yourself over to God, you will limit what He can do for you, and His perfect will and plan for your life. It's important for you to find a bible-based, Holy Spirit-filled church, get prayed up, prayed over, and lifted up with prayers as you get ready to battle in Jesus' name. My wife began to share with me that I was going through a medical miracle and I needed to trust in God. She was correct. God had stabilized my weight loss and my body from further deterioration. As doctors expected the worst in my condition, the numbers begin to hold. The more my wife prayed, the more I believed God was speaking to her. Her faith in God's word and its application increased significantly during this time. She spoke words of encouragement that were so timely it felt like they were directly from God to me. He built our faith up while He was doing a work in each of us.

Desperate Measures

On the medical front, it was time for me to explore an alternative solution, so I turned to a local integrated provider that offered alternative methods to healing. My experience at the local holistic clinic was not a positive one. After the initial consultation by the medical doctor, the finance manager walked in to list the cost of each package, ranging in the thousands of dollars. Soon after purchasing a package, I was passed around among naturopathic doctors and that's when the mistakes started to happen. Simple things like lack of familiarity with my file and prescribing medication that contained ingredients harmful to my liver. There was also a breakdown in communication between physicians.

By this time, I had lost all confidence in their professional services. The worst part about the experience was trying to get a straight answer to my questions. It felt like a guessing game. It became clear that I had to do my own research to get answers. I decided to use some of their other services, such as IV treatments and infrared sauna, and to pursue an integrative liver specialist elsewhere. I was so tired of being in the dark and sitting in one appointment after another feeling like "this doctor is clueless," that I started to search online for a liver specialist.

I found a liver specialist in New Mexico in several online articles and on YouTube. He had been treating patients with conditions similar to mine, and worse, for decades. My wife and I packed up the SUV and headed out to New Mexico for our first appointment with him. We traveled about 21 hours and stayed at a nearby hotel for two weeks to receive treatments. We decided not to fly to avoid the health risks due to ascites and varices, and the limited medical services available at 30,000 feet in the air.

When we finally arrived at the clinic, we met so many nice people in the waiting room. People from all over the world travel to seek treatment there. Some of these people were given the worst imaginable diagnosis and told to go home. Traditional methods of treatment, and their doctors, failed them. We were blessed to meet such a kind and caring doctor and staff there. Clinics like this one offer a community of hope and a place for patients to connect with other patients. It is truly a unique place where long-term friendships are made.

As I finished up my IV treatments, I had to get drained yet again, this time at a hospital in New Mexico. As you can imagine, I was on the edge since I had never been drained there, but I had no choice. Each time I had a paracentesis done, I risked internal bleeding, injury to a blood vessel, organ puncture, and infection of the blood stream to an already weakened body. Let me tell you, God is faithful! In all of the 35 or more paracentesis, He was with me and kept me free from internal bleeding, injury, puncture, and infection - that alone was a miracle!

I had no idea back then who Pastor Jentezen Franklin was,

50

or that two years later I would be going through the School of Discipleship program and attending Free Chapel as well. I just knew that the church was too far away so I began watching his sermons on YouTube along with Pastor Joel Osteen and Pastor Joseph Prince. As good as the sermons were, I still needed to find a local church closer to home where I could also receive the laying on of hands.

World Harvest Church

My journey for physical healing eventually led me to The World Harvest Church of Roswell, GA. The truth is, had I not been diagnosed with this disease I probably would not have found Pastor Mirek Hufton and World Harvest Church. It took a trip to New Mexico, where I made two new friends at the clinic, Tom and Woody, to make the link back home in Georgia to WHC. Tom introduced me to Woody and they both began to pray over me. We have stayed in touch by phone or text and lift each other up in prayer regularly.

On our drive back to Atlanta, I recalled something Woody had told me about a pastor in the area by the name of Jentezen Franklin. Several weeks later, I felt the Lord reveal to me that my ascites is my mountain and that by faith I can command it to move! All day the word "revelation" stuck with me. Since my wife and I didn't have a home church, we paid our tithes on Tuesday to Samaritan's Purse and to the Christian Broadcasting Network (CBN). On Wednesday we visited WHC for the first time.

Pastor Mirek happened to be teaching on the book of Revelation and that night mentioned the name Jentezen Franklin, and Samaritan's Purse. Three signs that immediately caught my attention. By the end of the service, WHC felt like home to us. We were greeted by so many loving and caring people from the congregation, we immediately felt the love of Christ all around the church. Pastor Mirek laid hands on me and spoke healing and life over me. He also prophesied that a ministry would be born from my situation. I also remember Pastor Willie praying for me at one of the altar calls and soon after that calling me "man of God." My faith continued to be built up.

Healing Ministry

The church also has a healing ministry that is led by John and Mary, dedicated to loving on people and praying for healing for each person in need, which we attended on a regular basis. I found refuge there and the presence of God and His love for me. We were in the right place. Whether at church, in healing service, or in a small group class, we were surrounded by people filled with the Holy Ghost, an army of prayer warriors devoted to seeing me through my situation. I'm thankful that Pastor Mirek tells it how it is. He believes in the whole bible as God inspired and his sermons reflect that—real and not watered down, feel-good verses that itching ears want to hear to support their current standing in the Lord. We are fed meat and not bird seed and my situation required this level of intensity and the compassion of God's word.

The outpouring of love, compassion, and excitement from Pastor Mirek, and the warm reception from the congregation was—and still is—an absolutely incredible experience. At WHC the majority of my family who had moved to Georgia got baptized in water a few months later. Since attending this church, we have grown so much in our relationship with God, His Son, and the Holy Spirit.

Casa Paternal Church

During our trip to Florida to visit my father, my brother, Pastor Luis Medina, invited us to visit his church, Casa Paternal of Kissimmee, Florida. We went later in the week on a Thursday night, when the worship band got together to practice. During one of the praise songs, my brother asked if he and his church members could lay hands on my wife and I and pray over us. We accepted the invite since often when people prayed over us, we would sense an intense heat come over us and we could not hold back our tears. It was very difficult not to get emotional and weep as we were completely overwhelmed by God's love and presence. That night was no different, we were completely touched once again.

Prophecies

A man and a woman, named Christian and Carmen, in Casa Paternal that night prophesied over both of us in Spanish. The man said he saw a stamp of God over my body and within two months, my body would begin to reject medical treatments. What he didn't know was that a few days prior, I was let go from my job and my health insurance was set to expire in two months. I had not shared this information with anyone, including my dad or brother, and certainly not the man or woman since we had never met them before they laid hands on us.

As the disease progressed, it became difficult to hold down a job due to the time off needed for weekly procedures and albumin IV treatments. I had burned through my sick, personal, and vacation time faster than I was able to accumulate it.

Wouldn't you know it, the very next paracentesis a week later, I began leaking water and had to call it in as it had never happened to me before. The nurse coordinator on-call looked up in system and confirmed no record of issues. She said to keep applying pressure to keep the water from leaking out, so I did for the next few hours. After that, each paracentesis became increasingly more and more difficult as my body began to reject every catheter on each side of my stomach. The nurses were running out of ideas to drain fluid out of my body.

Two months after the night at Casa Paternal, I was approved for a Transjugular Intrahepatic Portosystemic Shunt (TIPS) surgery. My last paracentesis was one week after the TIPS procedure, and it was quite a traumatic experience. My peritoneum had gotten so scarred from the previous 35 paracentesis that procedure took getting stuck twice, one on each side, and a couple of catheters to try and penetrate my peritoneum. When catheters failed to work, I remember the nurse having to call the doctor on shift to assist. I don't recall seeing so many people in the room and a shift doctor in any of my previous paracentesis procedures.

The woman prophesied she could see someone had given me a gift with yellow on it and I needed to find it and discard it. My wife and I searched our condo until we found it and threw it away. In fact, we cleaned the house of anything suspect along the lines of what she revealed to us. I'm very thankful for Pastor Medina and his church and the love and support they have shown to us. I am forever grateful for the continual lifting us up in prayer. I look forward to going back and visiting my family at Casa Paternal.

A Hope and A Future

Not only did I need a physical detox, but I needed a spiritual detox as well, as my daughter-in-law would say. World Harvest Church of Roswell, Georgia, and my brother's church, Casa Paternal in Kissimmee, Florida, both helped me walk through my healing process during a very critical and difficult time in my life. I am thankful for the everlasting love of a forgiving Heavenly Father, a loving and caring family beginning with my wife and sons, the pastors that God brought into our lives, and the new church family of believers that we are a part of, both here in Georgia and in Florida.

Although every person will have to walk through their own valley, it's important to remember that God is in control and He has the final say, not the doctors. God is the final authority over you! Thank God for doctors, He uses them and medicine to help heal the body, but it was important for me to keep things in perspective that God can do what doctors cannot do. One of the challenges of living with end-stage liver cirrhosis and being a believer in Christ, was my understanding of what is a miracle versus what is a modern-day medical intervention. We tend to have a preference when it comes to how to receive a miracle or be healed. In my painful situation, I would pray to God to heal me and give me the miracle and not the medical solution. As I would learn later in my journey, I was trying to tell God when and how to heal me. It is easy to think of what we want and seldom think of what God wants from us and to do through us.

Step Out in Faith

At the time, I didn't consider a person who needed a medical treatment miraculously healed. If you listen closely, you can hear the pride of a man not willing to surrender his disease and will completely over to God. Yet, it wasn't until I made the decision to step out on faith and be healed according to God's will and not my own, that physical healing came. One thing my journey of faith has taught me is to give thanks always to God for who He is and what He does. He has so much more to offer to those who love and serve Him.

His purpose for you is to be healed and walk in perfect health. To give you a future and a hope so that you can serve Him. He has a perfect will for each of us that is more beneficial and profitable than our own. If you wrote your idea of a perfect plan down on paper, His plan for you is still better. The promise of His Holy Spirit as our Comforter to help us, is available today, just as our Lord and Savior Jesus Christ of Nazareth said.

His Spirit leads us in truth, in power, and in wisdom. We cannot tell God what to do or when to do it, but we can change from our own ways and get back to living in His perfect will. We can also stand on His word by faith and let Him know every now and then that we have sown seed in the ground.

It's never too late for God to show up, regardless how dismal the medical report may be or how painful the disease you are going through is, the more desperate the situation, the greater the opportunity for His power to be demonstrated and His name to be glorified. When you have come to the end of yourself you will know that only God is at work (not you). He has the final say over your life, not anyone else—not the doctors, priests, pastors, relatives, friends, or co-workers.

No other power can rival God's Word. No other power can snatch you from the grip of God. His love for you is unconditional and His word will not return void. There is nothing you can do to earn God's love for you, to make Him love you more, or love you any less. He is faithful unto Himself and His word.

Don't just do these steps with the goal of being healed, do these steps to build a personal relationship with God, to embrace Him for who He is and what He does. He is our Heavenly Father and our Redeemer in Jesus' name. Use your current situation, no matter how painful the valley may be, to learn more about Him and His will for you. In the process, get all the blessings and promises you can from God, and don't limit yourself. God can provide above and beyond what you ask for and exceed your expectations when you ask according to His will.

Start Where You Are

You will need to begin somewhere, so start right where you are. I have documented for you my journey of faith, including my personal challenges and how they were addressed, going from being diagnosed with an end-stage disease to living for God in the name of Jesus Christ. The following section will help you build your faith, using the lessons I learned, if you follow God and get real with Him. Keep an open mind and be willing to change for the better.

Give Thanks

The words we speak have more power than we realize. Equally important to the words we choose is how we communicate those words to others. I didn't always understand this, I was more interested in proving my point of view than in how I treated others or made them feel. The tongue has the power to bring comfort or conflict into every situation. People don't always remember what you say, but how you made them feel when you said it.

When it comes to faith, a person will either increase or decrease their level of faith by their own words. We can speak life and seal the outcome of a situation or speak death and set the course for the future. Each individual gets to determine what words to choose and whether those words will speak a blessing or a curse into his or her life. Proverbs 18:21 tells us that "Death and life are in the power of the tongue, and those who love it will eat its fruit." Proverbs 12:18 reminds us, "The words of the reckless pierce like swords, but the tongue of the wise brings healing" (NIV).

Sometimes it is not easy to give thanks to God when you

are going through a difficult season in your life. The primary thought on our minds is not always to give thanks to God but to instead think about ourselves and how to get out of the situation. Giving thanks to God was not my first thought either, but it has now become a constant state of mind and daily expression to be thankful and give God thanks even for a drink of water.

With the passing of each day that I woke up still alive, and not six feet under, I began to realize that God is a good God and a God of second chances. I had much to be thankful for. 1 Thessalonians 5:18 says, "In everything give thanks; for this is the will of God in Christ Jesus for you" (KJV). There are many people in the United States and across the world in worse condition, remember that. The 139th chapter of the book of Psalms says in verse 13, "For you created my inmost being; you knit me together in my mother's womb" (NIV). Recognizing who God is, accepting by faith how He created you, and giving Him thanks are absolutely essential to turning things around.

When we start to give thanks to God, our attention is on Him and what He can do instead of on us and what we lack or can't do. We focus not on our weakness but on God' supernatural ability. Not only did God create and form each of us, He also loves His creation unconditionally and sent His most precious gift, His only begotten Son, Jesus Christ, to die on the cross at Calvary for our sins. John 3:16 reminds us, "For God so loved the world that he gave his one and only Son, that whoever believes in him shall not perish but have eternal life" (NIV).

Be Real with God

To be real with God means that one must be real with themselves first. We have to acknowledge where we are in life and
why we need Him. When I was first diagnosed, I didn't have
a clue about the disease called end-stage liver cirrhosis. My
immediate thoughts were, *Why me God? Why would you do
this to me?* I was angry with God. There was a part of me that
wanted to believe He was a kill-joy God and not for me. That
He didn't love me or care about me. He was not into the details
of my life. I was not worthy of His love.

I blamed God for everything bad that was happening to
me. Even in my critical condition, my eyes were still fixed
on me and not on God and His grace. I was looking at things
through my limited lens. This all began to change when my
son Matt invited me to church one Sunday morning. An artist
named Matt Redman was the guest artist singing that Sunday
morning and he sang a song called "Gracefully Broken" during
worship. The lyrics captivated my heart. It was then I realized
God had spared my life and was using this awful situation to
gracefully put me back together for a greater purpose. I could

have just keeled over and died from a heart attack in the gym, like I had heard happened to a guy earlier. But by the grace of God, I didn't and was still here for a second chance.

It's okay to vent our anger and frustration with God because He is real. There is nothing we can say to Him that He doesn't already know. He knows the outcome from the present condition. Our future from our past. He's the same yesterday, today, and forever. When we speak with Him, we can speak from the heart because He's not impressed by many words. Always be respectful when speaking to God because He is holy and faithful. Psalm 89:7 reminds us, "God is greatly to be feared in the assembly of the saints, And to be held in reverence by all those around Him." Humility goes a long way with God. It's important to repent of any pride we have and humble ourselves, for He is faithful and shows mercy to those who humble themselves. He is not a kill-joy God as I once thought. He wants to grant us the desires of our hearts according to His will.

When I realized that God is for me, it gave me great hope and comfort in knowing that He is not against me. Nothing can separate me from His love, and there is nothing I can do to increase or decrease His unconditional love for me. Friends may let you down; some of your family members may even let you down at times; but God promises He will never leave you nor forsake you. He is faithful and will be with you where your family cannot be. His presence goes before and with you when your life is in the hands of a doctor. He is above everyone who is above you.

Surrender Your All

To truly surrender our all, we must cease resistance and submit to God's authority. We must deny ourselves and trust God and His perfect will for each of us. He is either Lord of all in your life or Lord of none. He's not a second-place God. He is the author and finisher of our faith. Giving up control is never easy to do, especially for a person who feels the need to be in control of every situation. If you are anything like me this will be an area of struggle at first, but it is critical that you work on it and get past this step. Giving up control means we are trusting in God's supernatural ability and not our own strength and understanding.

We can go to war against the disease on our own and try to defend ourselves, or we can hand it over to God and let Him defend and lead us to victory. In the book of Matthew chapter 10, verse 1, it says that Jesus "gave them power over unclean spirits, to cast them out, and to heal all kinds of sickness and all kinds of disease." Not all battles are fought in the physical world. God created us in His image, and we are more than just a body: We are spirit, soul, and body.

Just like we have laws by which we operate in the physical realm, there are also laws that exist in the spiritual realm. Ephesians 6:12 says, "For we do not wrestle against flesh and blood, but against principalities, against powers, against the rulers of the darkness of this age, against spiritual hosts of wickedness in the heavenly places." This is noteworthy because if it was important enough for the Apostle Paul to address this in the earlier days, then it should be even more significant today given the proliferation of sin and disease that exists in the world.

Like when one breaks the law there are consequences to pay, the same holds true in the spiritual realm. When a person sins and does not truly repent to God, they open themselves up and give legal right for spiritual attacks from spirits of darkness on their body, soul, and spirit. Being a Christian doesn't make one immune from these attacks, especially if one practices sin on an ongoing basis.

There is more happening than what is visible in the physical realm. The only one who can break that legal right and restore a person to salvation and health is God. This is why it's so important we surrender everything to God. There is power in the blood of Christ to break the bondage of sin and set us free, but we cannot do it alone.

Trust in God

It took a while, but I learned I didn't have to go through this journey alone. I turned to my Heavenly Father, Who formed me, and relinquished my disease to Him. I began to study His word and created a list of promises that helped me overcome many painful procedures and low days. I had to trust in God, that He is the same yesterday, today, and forever, and not trust in my feelings alone.

Promises like, God loves me, He is always with me, He takes care of me, He heals me, and He will never leave me nor forsake me, all made the top of my God's promise list. I would often meditate on this list as I waited for another appointment or procedure. God's word also helped me know that God was right there with me and could see my tears and feel my pain. My trust in God continues to grow daily.

To trust God, it takes a firm belief in the reliability of who He is and in the truth of His word (the scriptures). In Psalm 18:30 David says, "As for God, His way is perfect; The word of the Lord is proven; He is a shield to all who trust in Him." It takes faith to accept God as the Lord of one's life, and obedience to maintain an ongoing relationship with Him. Often when bad things happen, such as a natural disaster or an unexpected disease, we tend to blame God for it. The truth is that according to 2 Corinthians 4:4, "Satan, who is the god of this world, has blinded the minds of those who don't believe. They are unable to see the glorious light of the Good News. They don't understand this message about the glory of Christ, who is the exact likeness of God." Since sin entered the world through Adam and Eve's disobedience in the garden, we can expect satan, who has been granted power to rule over the air, is working overtime to pervert the word of God, steal God's word from you, destroy your testimony, kill your body, and deceive as many people as possible.

Luke 4:3-6 says,

Then the devil said to him, 'If you are the Son of God, tell this stone to become a loaf of bread." But Jesus told him, "No! The Scriptures say, 'People do not live by bread alone.' Then the devil took him up and revealed to him all the kingdoms of the world in a moment of time. "I will give you the glory of these kingdoms and authority over them," the devil said, "because they are mine to give to anyone I please" (NLT).

If Jesus Who never sinned was tempted, how much more should we who have sinned expect to be tempted? Jesus was faithful to God the Father even unto death on the cross for our sins and for all time. He knew and quoted the scriptures when tempted, which is an exemplary model for us to follow. Trust in God to defend and fight for you against all your struggles in life. In order to quote the word, you must study the word.

Jesus, Lord and Savior

Making the decision to accept Jesus as my Lord and Savior was—and still is—a life-changing experience. It was an easy decision for me to make given the challenges I had growing up without my biological father. Although I was raised by my mom and stepdad (who did the best he could with what he had), I always felt there was something missing in my life. It has been some 30 years now and I have not forgotten my trip to visit my biological father as a young adult just after I got married. By that time, I had only seen him a handful of times throughout my life.

I remember when my biological father witnessed to me about Jesus one night as we talked. He shared how he had everything he wanted in life, yet he still felt a "hole in his heart" that no material thing (e.g., house, cars, horses, job title, etc.) could fulfill until he gave his life over to Jesus. My father had accepted Christ as his personal Lord and Savior and left an everlasting impression on me. Upon returning home to Massachusetts, I immediately began visiting different churches in search of one to call home.

I had been raised as a catholic believer all my life, yet I was yearning for something more. I was also trying to fill a hole in my heart and didn't realize it at the time. Within a couple of months, I had found a Pentecostal church, The Lowell Assembly of God in Tewksbury, MA, and accepted the same Jesus Christ as my Lord and Savior that my earthly father had shared with me in Puerto Rico.

When you think of all our Heavenly Father has done for us, why would anyone hesitate or resist the invitation to accept His only begotten Son, Jesus? First John 4:9 says, "In this the love of God was manifested toward us, that God has sent His only begotten Son into the world, that we might live through Him." Jesus Who was sinless became the ultimate sacrifice on the cross for our sins. He bore not just all our sins, but our sorrow, sickness, and so much more.

Isaiah 53:4 reminds us that Jesus,

Bore our griefs and carried our sorrows; yet we esteemed Him stricken, smitten by God, and afflicted. But He was wounded for our transgressions, He was bruised for our iniquities; the chastisement for our peace was upon Him, and by His stripes we are healed. All we like sheep have gone astray; we have turned, every one, to his own way; And the Lord has laid on Him the iniquity of us all.

It was a great comfort to know Jesus fully understood my pain and could identify with what I was going through. His body was broken so that my body might be made whole again. He was stricken so that by His stripes I may be healed. Philippians 1:20 says, "According to my earnest expectation and hope that in nothing I shall be ashamed, but with all boldness, as always, so now also Christ will be magnified in my body, whether by life or by death. For to me, to live is Christ, and to die is gain."

Christ by Baptism

I can't think of a better public confession after receiving Jesus Christ as Lord and Savior than being baptized in the Holy Spirit in complete immersion. It is such a personal and emotional step of identifying with Christ in death and in the new resurrected life. Romans 6:4 says, "Therefore we were buried with Him through baptism into death, that just as Christ was raised from the dead by the glory of the Father, even so we also should walk in newness of life."

By now, I was beginning to see how God was graciously at work in my situation. He was not only restoring and healing me, but He was also at work healing my family. He was drawing all of us closer to Him and to each other. How often do you get to see your wife, son, and his wife baptized at the same time in the name of Jesus? That's what happened when each one of us who was willing, surrendered all to Christ as Lord and Savior. We were baptized and rededicated our lives to God.

All of a sudden, I went from fearing death on the night of August 29, 2017, to having peace and knowing that no matter what happens, I belong to my Lord Jesus Christ. My prayer request of only wanting the miracle and not the medical treatment changed. I began to consider modern-day procedures and medicine as a tool used by God. As much as I had reservations about how to be healed, I had to let this area of pride go and fully release it to God. Now, regardless of what happened, I was to humble myself before God and accept His will for how He wanted to heal and restore me. Each of the steps, from giving thanks to getting baptized in the Holy Spirit, have played a critical role in my healing process spiritually, and in returning to God.

The Holy Spirit

The Holy Spirit has become more important to me than ever
before. I began to understand that the Holy Spirit is an actual
person and not an abstract concept. He is God's promise to
help, comfort, and teach us in all things. I'm still learning to
be sensitive and listen to the Holy Spirit and His wisdom. I'm
also paying more attention to hearing Him speak through His
word, other believers, dreams, and that still, small voice.

First Corinthians 2:12-14 says,

> Now we have received, not the spirit of the world,
> but the Spirit who is from God, that we might know
> the things that have been freely given to us by God.
> These things we also speak, not in words which
> man's wisdom teaches but which the Holy Spirit
> teaches, comparing spiritual things with spiritual.
> But the natural man does not receive the things of
> the Spirit of God, for they are foolishness to him;
> nor can he know them, because they are spiritually
> discerned.

A couple of months after I had been diagnosed with end-stage liver cirrhosis, I got out of bed one night and fainted. According to my wife, I hit the floor so hard it woke her up. I don't remember anything other than her calling out my name over and over in a faint voice. I was in a deep sleep and, honestly, I could have stayed there. It was very peaceful. But I was awakened by her pushing on my body. I woke up to a bloody face and was taken to the emergency room by my wife, my son Matt, and his wife.

I'm thankful that earlier that morning I had been drained of about 15 lbs. of body fluid. I can't imagine what might have happened had I hit the floor with all that water around my waist. Although I had fallen hard and was weak physically, not one bone was broken, thank God. I'm not sure why, but I no longer wanted to sleep in what was practically a new bed with a special adjustable frame that cost thousands of dollars. The bed was just too high for me. I stopped sleeping on it for fear I would fall again.

My wife and I decided to hire a cleaning lady for the first time to clean our condo. Her name was Blanca, and she came highly recommended. We had not met this woman or her helper before. We were not used to anyone cleaning our condo, so it was somewhat awkward for us. While they were in one of the bathrooms cleaning, I went to the kitchen to make a snack. I felt pressed upon my heart to "Offer her the bed." I was taken back since I didn't know the lady and didn't want to offend her. I was hesitant at first. I was unsure how to approach her, but I just knew I had to ask her.

Just before she was about to leave, I asked her if she knew someone who would be interested in a bed with an adjustable frame. She immediately broke down in tears and wept as she shared with us that her youngest son has a disorder and she needed a special bed for him. Our bed was perfect for her little boy. Although I had no clue about her son, we were blessed by her. She is a Holy Spirit-filled woman of God who prayed for me along with my wife for healing and then had her church also lift us up in prayer when we visited the next day. We also got to meet her son.

Acts of Worship

The thought that God considers anyone who does not tithe to be a thief, and one who would rather steal from God than give a tenth of their income so that there may be meat in God's house, is a serious offense against God. Malachi 3:8 says, "Will a man rob God? Yet you have robbed Me! But you say, 'In what way have we robbed You?' In tithes and offerings." My wife and I have experienced first-hand the benefits of bringing our tithes and offerings to God's house, from the beginning when it seemed we could not begin to tithe, to being able to tithe what we earned in a month every year. God has always been faithful and never let us down.

God invites each of us to test Him in the area of giving of tithes and offerings. It's like an invitation to see if we think we can out-give God, Who owns everything. It's a challenge we will always lose. We will never out-do God but certainly win, as a result of God's promise and favor when we do our part. According to Malachi 3:10 when we are obedient with our portion, the Lord of hosts says He will "open for you the windows of heaven and pour out for you such a blessing that there will not be room enough to receive it." When you think of how God created the heavens and the earth and everything in it, including all the wealth, and how He promises to supply all our needs, why would anyone ever think to rob from God?

When we tithe, we acknowledge that God is our provider; we are putting the needs of others before our own needs; and we are positioning ourselves to receive a blessing so great that we will not have enough room to receive it. By bringing your tithes and offerings into God's house you are preparing to live under an open heaven that is full of every blessing you will ever need. When you tithe, it is an act of obedience and worship—an affair of the heart between you and your Creator.

In verse 11 of Malachi chapter 3, God also promises to "rebuke the devourer for your sake, so that he will not destroy the fruit of your ground, nor shall the vine fail to bear fruit for you in the field...says the Lord of hosts." I believe this promise also applies to your health. When you sow into God's kingdom by bringing your tithes and offerings to God's house, you have planted seed in the ground. That seed allows you to bring your sickness to God and claim all that He has in store for you.

Sowing seeds, standing on God's promises, being obedient to God, letting go of pride and unforgiveness, are all critical to receiving healing. But healing may not always happen according to our expectations or timeframe. Remember the cupbearer cried, fasted, prayed, confessed, and repented, and then reminded God of His mercy. God responded and gave Nehemiah favor to go and rebuild the walls. Your body is the temple of the Holy Spirit. Trust in God to rebuild and heal your broken body. It's only human to have a preconceived notion of how you would like God to heal you. I wanted God to heal me through a miracle and not with the use of any medical solution.

I was proud of the fact that I was approaching 50 years old and never had any type of medical procedure or surgery.

For over 6 months, I resisted and rejected the idea of having a TIPS medical procedure, as I waited for my miraculous healing. My decision to accept God's healing only through a miracle continued until Matt called me out on it. I'll never forget what he said that got me thinking. Did I want God to heal me according to my will or His? It became clear that I wanted God to heal me on my terms.

I had allowed pride to settle in the area of expectations and needed to repent and humble myself before God. It was keeping me from receiving my physical healing. Is it possible for God to miraculously heal someone today? Sure it is! He can also heal through doctors with the use of medicine and the medical advancements available today. The important thing is to always put your faith in God and not the doctors. My pastor also confirmed that I should take the medicine available to me but put my trust in God for the healing.

As I struggled to let go of control of how I wanted God to heal me, I had to completely trust in God for what would happen next. The TIPS procedure would be the first time I would subject myself to being sedated for 4 hours. The estimated duration of the procedure was 1-2 hours, but due to the complexity of my situation it took the doctors up to 4 hours to finish. Another thing Matt said that resonated with me was to view laying down my body for the procedure as an act of worship. This was a game changer because it helped me realize I could do more than stand in faith on God's word, I could also, with complete trust, present my body before God as an act of worship.

No matter what health crisis you or your loved one may

be going through, hope awaits you. As difficult as the situation may seem, use this time to discover God's plan and purpose for you. Jeremiah 29:11 reminds us what God wants for us, "For I know the plans I have for you says the Lord...to give you a future and a hope." Grab on to these and other promises from God that specifically deal with you, your blessings, your healing, and your future. You'll find that God is able to heal you in more ways than you can imagine.

God's Promise List

I don't remember the exact moment when I decided to jot down promises from God, but I recall having a hunger for guarantees in life that would help me cope with my valley. All of a sudden, God's promises started jumping out at me during church, watching sermons online, and when reading the Bible. There were so many promises I created a list on my phone and began adding to the list over time.

Little did I know then that this same promise list would serve to encourage and help others dealing with their own medical crisis. As I shared with other patients and medical professionals how God's promise list had helped me in my situation, they would ask me to send my list to their phones. God's promises became my guarantee in life and the building blocks for new hope and a future. My Lord and Savior Jesus Christ became my Redeemer. This promise list was so important to me I would often read the promises out loud before my appointments. The atmosphere would begin to change almost instantly. The list helped me take my attention away from my personal needs and the stress of anticipating another paracentesis and focus on my Redeemer instead!

God's word would transform me from a victim mentality into a warrior state-of-mind, ready to let Jesus shine through. Prior to having the promise list, I felt alone and as though nobody understood what I was going through or the pain I was feeling. This all changed with God's promise list. I gained knowledge about God and His promises that I did not know before. The promise list is more than just a list to help you get through your physical healing. The list is a reminder of all that God is and what He can do for you to heal you spiritually and emotionally as well. If all you seek is a physical healing, then you will short-change yourself and miss out on the greater works of God in your life. The list is designed to comfort you and give you victory in the midst of your sickness. Victory comes in many forms and begins with your heart and attitude towards God and others as you confront and live through the disease.

My prayer for you is that God's word will go to work for you in the midst of your darkest valley. More important than the promise list itself is that you gain a deeper understanding of God's everlasting love for you; how God is for you and not against you; and how nothing is impossible with God. We can do all things through Christ who strengthens us, even during our walk through a valley.

God Loves Me

Growing up in a different religion in New England, I remembered hearing about God but not about His love for me, or that He cared enough to want a relationship with me. Not much thought was given to Him at the time other than He was some ancient God in a distant world no longer relevant in our daily living, and certainly not concerned with the details of one's daily life. The church we attended on some occasions was purely about the practice of their religion.

To this day, I don't understand how God forbids us to create an image and worship it, yet that was exactly what the church did by creating statues of saints and praying to them. That religion also elevated Mary's role above the position of Jesus, which is also something I don't understand. None of that taught me it was possible to have a personal relationship with God through His Son, Jesus.

As I began to learn the truth about God, I felt like a hypocrite at times because although the Bible taught me that God is love, I still had doubts about God's love for me. I also had trouble reconciling my version of faith based on performing

my way to God and believing by seeing, with God's defini-
tion of faith—Things hoped for without the evidence of being
seen. Saying you believe in something and actually living it
are two different things. It was easier for me to say I believed
in what I could see than it was to believe in what I couldn't see.

What I felt was real, although not visible to the eye. For
example, the love one has for his or her spouse, earthly father,
mother, siblings, sons, or daughters. You know your love is
real and nobody can tell you otherwise, because you feel it.
One can see and know the measure of that love based on the
affection and demonstration of love. Our Heavenly Father's
agape love for us is a higher form of love, it's sacrificial. He
demonstrates His love for us through the finished work of
Christ. His love does not seek its own. We cannot perform our
way to earn God's love. Our daily fellowship with God must
be based on spending time in His word and not just on feelings
or what is visible. We need to live by faith in the power of the
Holy Spirit to reveal areas of our souls that need to be under
the Lordship of Jesus!

First John 4:8-10 says, "He who does not love does not
know God, for God is love. In this the love of God was manifested toward us, that God has sent His only begotten Son into
the world, that we might live through Him. In this is love, not
that we loved God, but that He loved us and sent His Son to
be the propitiation for our sins." First Corinthians 13:1-2 tells
us, "Though I speak with the tongues of men and of angels,
but have not love, I have become sounding brass or a clanging
cymbal. And though I have the gift of prophecy, and understand all mysteries and all knowledge, and though I have all
faith, so that I could remove mountains, but have not love, I
am nothing."

The Father that Jesus referred to in the Bible is more than just an ancient God, He is the one true, living God Who created all things, first loved us, knows us intimately, and has a perfect will for each of us. He is still relevant in His world today and cares very much about your future.

God is with Me

A quick and guaranteed way to isolate yourself and feel lonely is to take your eyes off God and remove yourself from His hand of protection over your life. It's just a matter of time when you subject yourself to spiritual attacks, whether you believe it or not. You'll even try to replace your emptiness with temporary fixes and end up in bondage until you come to the end of yourself.

But thanks be to God that He is a God of second chances and of mercy and grace. We have all fallen short of the glory of God and need His forgiveness and protection. God promises if we return to Him, He will return to us. We have to truly humble ourselves, sincerely repent of our sins, truly accept Jesus as our personal Savior if we haven't already, and ask God for His forgiveness, mercy, and grace.

A true return to God means a true change of heart, making a 180-degree turn, and not living the old way you used to. Zechariah 1:3 says, "Therefore say to them, 'Thus says the Lord of hosts: "Return to Me and I will return to you," says the Lord of hosts.'" Isaiah 41:10 tells us to, "Fear not, for I am with you; be not dismayed, for I am your God; I will strengthen you, I will help you, I will uphold you with my righteous right hand" (ESV).

Joshua 1:9 reminds us to, "Be strong and courageous. Do not be frightened, and do not be dismayed, for the Lord your God is with you wherever you go." God's promise to forgive me and to always be with me gave me the assurance that I was no longer walking through this sickness alone. To know that God is love, loves me endlessly, created me in His image, and delights in His creation, offers hope and a higher standard of worth than any professional or doctor can offer. Remember, God is over those who are over you and surrounds those who surround you. You have nothing to fear, God is with you.

God Takes Care of Me

Letting go of old habits and making room for God to take care of us, when for most of our lives, we are used to making our own decisions, is not easy. It didn't take long after the disease struck for me to begin worrying about the quality of my health and my life. There were many nights when I wasn't sure I would wake up the following morning. The night the doctor asked me if I needed to speak with a priest or pastor worried me.

That question would invade my thoughts as often as I would let it. I worried about how we would pay the medical bills that were stacking up one by one. But God had another plan for us! He did not want us to be in debt or to worry about anything. In less than one year, we were debt free except for a mortgage and car payment.

When we worry, it's like saying we don't believe God is capable to provide for all our needs. The scriptures remind us just how faithful God is and how He wants to take care of us.

Therefore I say to you, do not worry about your life, what you will eat or what you will drink; nor about your body, what you will put on. Is not life more than food and the body more than clothing? Look at the birds of the air, for they neither sow nor reap nor gather into barns; yet your heavenly Father feeds them. Are you not of more value than they? Which of you by worrying can add one cubit to his stature?

Matthew 6:25

Therefore, the next time you feel the need to worry, don't. Take the attention off yourself and begin to praise and give glory to God! Thank Him for Who He is and what He does! Thank God, for all the promises in Him are yes and amen in Christ Jesus! Thank God that you are the head and not the tail; you are blessed going in and blessed coming out; you are to lend and not borrow; and you are to live and not die.

Do not yield submission to your disease, not even for a minute! Give glory to God for we have been bought by Christ with His blood and we are more than conquerors by the blood of the Lamb, and by the word of their testimony! God is faithful and His word will not return void! His plan is to prosper you, not harm you, and give you a hope and a future.

God Heals Me

God heals in more ways and for different reasons than you and I can imagine or think. Our urgent prayer request and what we think is a real priority may not be God's top priority for us. We may place a demand or obligation on God in prayer, but it's not about our will but His will being done. It's not about our timeframe either. Some healings are delayed because they will serve a greater purpose. In John 11:4 Jesus said, "This sickness is not unto death, but for the glory of God, that the Son of God may be glorified through it." God is not bound by time and space as we are.

Our purview of God's perfect will and purpose for our life is at best, limited in scope, so we must continue to trust in Him for our healing. We must trust His plan and future for us even when we don't understand His reasons or timing. He may use your healing as a reason for others to believe and see the glory of God through His Son, Jesus.

God's timing for healing us is His and not ours to begin with, and certainly not according to how or when we think the healing should happen. Jesus could have raised Lazarus the minute he heard the news, but He had a greater purpose to reveal to everyone standing by. John 11:25-26 reminds us who Jesus is, "I am the resurrection and the life. He who believes in Me, though he may die, he shall live. And whoever lives and believes in Me shall never die. Do you believe this?"

Later, in the book of John chapter 11, verses 40-43, Jesus says,

> Did I not say to you that if you would believe you would see the glory of God?....Jesus lifted up His eyes and said, "Father, I thank You that You have heard Me. And I know that You always hear Me, but because of the people who are standing by I said this, that they may believe that You sent Me." Now when He had said these things, He cried with a loud voice, "Lazarus, come forth!"

So Lazarus who was alive then dead was raised by Jesus for all, including those close to Him, to witness the resurrection power of our Lord, Christ.

There may come a time when it seems the sickness is winning but don't be discouraged, for God is in control and able to heal all diseases. There isn't a disease God can't heal or a situation where He is late or runs out of time. It's important not to embrace your sickness and instead focus on God and His sovereignty. Look for the spiritual lessons as you walk through your dark valley.

God Orders My Steps

My God knows the outcome from the beginning. He knows your future from the present. He is in control and is strategic in His plans for you. Although you may make plans in your heart, the steps of a good man are ordered by the Lord. Psalm 37:23 reminds us, "The steps of a good man are ordered by the Lord, And He delights in his way." There is nowhere you can run to or hide that the Lord God can't find you.

There is no situation too big or too small that the Lord can't give you a way out, a future and a hope. The doors He opens no one can close, the one He closes no one can open. The book of Revelation 3:7 says the Lord holds the key not us, "These are the words of the One who is holy and true, who holds the key of David. What He opens, no one will shut; and what He shuts, no one will open."

Whatever plans you made before falling into your sickness, turn it around, begin to align your will with God's will and perfect plan for your life. You will begin to see God's hand at work in your situation. Don't give up but press in, especially when it doesn't make sense.

God Will Never Leave Me Nor Forsake Me

The more I read God's word, the more He comforted me. I found great peace in knowing that regardless of my inadequacy to deal with my medical situation, He was with me and would not fail me. The book of Deuteronomy 31:6 reminds us to, "Be strong and of good courage, do not fear nor be afraid of them; for the Lord your God, He is the One who goes with you. He will not leave you nor forsake you."

You too can have the assurance that the God of Abraham, Isaac, and Jacob, will never leave you nor forsake you. Return to Him and He will return to you! He is also the God of generational blessings. Blessings that don't just apply to you, but apply to your children, and to your grandchildren, and so forth.

Sometimes, you may not feel God's presence as strong as you do other days but know that your relationship with Him is not based on what you feel, but on His word. Study His word and take hold of all the promises and blessings He has in store for you. Honor the Lord your God with all your possessions and be ready for every good work.

Like Joshua, make a bold declaration, "As for me and my

house, we will serve the Lord."

> And if it seems evil to you to serve the Lord, choose for yourselves this day whom you will serve, whether the gods which your fathers served that were on the other side of the river, or the gods of the Amorites, in whose land you dwell. But as for me and my house, we will serve the Lord.

Joshua 24:15

God Is Faithful

God is still faithful even when we don't understand what is happening and are faithless. Second Timothy 2:13 says, "If we are faithless, he remains faithful—for he cannot deny himself." One cold winter afternoon just before I was about to leave work, I noticed my feet had swelled up pretty badly with fluid. The swelling made it nearly impossible to stand, let alone walk. The walk from my office to the parking garage was absolutely excruciating.

As I took each step towards my car, it felt like there was a 20-pound block of ice on each foot. The more I walked, the more painful it got. Finally, after I arrived home, I could no longer hold the pain inside and began to cry out loud to the Lord, "Heal me Lord, or give me relief." This cry was very different, it was nothing like the other ones; it was deep, from the soul. My wife laid hands on me and prayed over me and a short while later I received my relief!

LUIS MEDINA

2 Corinthians 12:9-10 tells us,

But he said to me, 'My grace is sufficient for you, for my power is made perfect in weakness.' Therefore I will boast all the more gladly about my weaknesses, so that Christ's power may rest on me. That is why, for Christ's sake, I delight in weaknesses, in insults, in hardships, in persecutions, in difficulties. For when I am weak, then I am strong.

When I was on the table about to undergo a medical procedure, God was over all those present in the room. If you ask Him to, He will even go before you and set the table for you. He will protect you in the midst of the darkest valley of your life. If you bring your tithes and offerings to His house, He will rebuke the devourer for you. All you have to do is ask and live according to His will.

God's Plans for Me Are for Good

The book of Romans 8:28 says, "And we know that all things work together for good to those who love God, to those who are the called according to His purpose."

I wish I had shared what I was experiencing non-stop every night for over 6 months with my pastor and my pastor brother sooner. I would wake up in massive pain with my legs cramping and sometimes the cramps were so intense I would cry out for help. My feet would start to curl, and I would lock up from the waist down. This happened at all hours throughout the night and into the morning, especially between 2 a.m. and 3 a.m. and would stop by 6 a.m. Looking back now, there was more going on than just a physical condition.

Sometimes, I would not be able to move as I stood in place and waited about 20 minutes before the pain subsided. Other times, I would lose my balance and hit the floor. I tried everything: stretching to get rid of lactic acid, drinking coconut water for electrolytes, taking magnesium supplements, eating potassium-rich vegetables, increasing sodium intake, and drinking more water to rule out dehydration. It didn't matter what I did, night after night, the same thing happened over and over again.

Little did I know then there is such a thing as a spiritual attack, and that the hour between 2 a.m. and 3 a.m. is a door some people use to do witchcraft. It wasn't until I visited my dad and stayed over at his place for three nights that I realized I had slept with no interruptions and no cramps. I shared this with my dad and brother before heading back home. This got my attention because working in the Information Technology field, I looked for patterns when troubleshooting issues.

Pastor Medina equipped us with knowledge and instructions for what we needed to do when we returned home. We arrived so tired from the trip we decided to go to sleep that night and follow his instructions in the morning. Like clockwork, the attack occurred again at about 2:38 a.m. My wife and I decided not to wait anymore and followed each step later that morning. We applied oil on every door and window entrance and cast out all unclean spirits in the name of Jesus. The attacks stopped immediately. It's been over two years now with no reoccurrence of attacks. I'm also back to exercising again.

I Shall Live and Not Die

Psalms 118:17 says, "I shall not die, but live, And declare the works of the Lord."

We started attending World Harvest Church of Roswell, where we immediately began to be fed the entire word of God. I'm talking about being fed steak and not bird seed. We learned about a healing class offered through the church and started attending. John and Mary led the healing ministry and on the first night we attended my wife and I began speaking in tongues.

One night as John and two other men laid hands on me and prayed, he felt the need to pray specifically for God to remove pain in my body while I slept. I was surprised to hear his prayer since I had never shared any of this with anyone at the church, including John! I think I was too proud and narrow-minded at the time.

I couldn't wait to attend the next church service. I remember the first person I went up to for prayer was pastor Willie. This is a man of God, who loves the Lord, and he and his wife are an inspiration to anyone looking to grow in faith and in ministry. I also looked for the opportunity to receive prayer from the senior pastor, Mirek. His sermons were so on point, so specific, so timely, that at times it was like God was speaking directly to us through him.

No one knew what we were dealing with each week except my wife and God. Then came the word of knowledge about how I had an anointing. It was intense. During service, Pastor Mirek would come over to deliver a prophetic word over me about how God would use our testimony. What a man of God, who has served the Lord faithfully for decades! Both he and his wife, pastor Linda, are an inspiration to living out the word of God. Pastor Mirek prophesied over me that I shall live and not die! I received it!

In Florida, Pastor Medina at Casa Paternal and his congregation were going to battle with us as well, lifting my family up in prayer and keeping us at the forefront of their minds during a critical time. Pastor Medina would constantly text me God's word and speak life over me. As the procedures intensified, my brother would also escalate and declare God's promises over us.

Also engaged in the battle were all those in our circle of faith and small group, and brothers and sisters in Christ. My wife, my sons, my daughter-in-law, were all pulling together for me and they were steadfast in calling and texting me words of encouragement at random times throughout the day and before every procedure. They were faithful and never gave up! We planted seed in the ground and stood on God's word and continued to trust in Him.

Bought with the Blood of Christ

I am not my own! You are not your own! For we have been purchased by the blood of the Lamb! We no longer live unto ourselves but unto our Lord Jesus, for our body is the temple of our comforter, the Holy Spirit, as promised by God. First Corinthians 6:19-20 reminds us of this, "Or do you not know that your body is the temple of the Holy Spirit who is in you, whom you have from God, and you are not your own? For you were bought at a price; therefore glorify God in your body and in your spirit, which are God's." No matter how desperate the situation, how devastating the news, or how discouraging the outcome appears, the disease is not your own. Release it to God and begin to discern His will and purpose for your life.

God has great love for you! He is bigger than the sickness and He is a merciful God. Romans 12:1–2 tells us to, "Present your bodies a living sacrifice, holy, acceptable to God, which is your reasonable service. And do not be conformed to this world, but be transformed by the renewing of your mind, that you may prove what is that good and acceptable and perfect will of God."

In the book of Ephesians, chapter 2, verse 4 says, "But God, being rich in mercy, because of the great love with which he loved us." This is a reminder that we have not only been bought at a price, but bought by a living God Who loves us with an everlasting love.

God's Word Will Not Return Void

God's word is not limited to one generation. His word works for every generation, including our present one. Isaiah 55:11 says, "So shall My word be that goes forth from My mouth; It shall not return to Me void, But it shall accomplish what I please, And it shall prosper in the thing for which I sent it." In the midst of your situation, you can know that the same God Who is for you and loves you, will not fail you. He can meet you right where you are.

Second Corinthians 5:17 reminds us, "Therefore, if anyone is in Christ, he is a new creation. The old has passed away; behold, the new has come." Begin to give thanks and praise to God for Who He is! Thank Him that He made you to be the head and not the tail, above and not beneath, blessed going in and blessed coming out, to lend and not borrow, to live and not die. Stand on the full power and authority of God's word. Look for God's healing in your life beyond just the physical. By Jesus' stripes we are healed. Our Heavenly Father's healing shall spring forth speedily.

My Life is in Your Hands, Lord

Being unexpectedly diagnosed with an end-stage disease can be extremely overwhelming. There is the sudden realization of a real threat to one's life; the gradual deterioration of one's health; the additional financial burdens, which appear to never end; the lifestyle changes and getting used to looking different; the diet restrictions; and the many limitations imposed by the sickness, just to name a few issues.

It's easy to get lost in all this while at the same time trying to be hopeful. All the medical information is delivered in a very technical manner and it's usually negative. We often focus on the worst-case scenario and if we are not careful, we can lose all hope and end up there, all alone, for a long time—all by our own choice.

In the beginning, it felt like my wife and I were walking under a constant dark cloud. I got tired of fighting this thing on my own. I wasn't as strong as I used to be physically, and there were days I just stayed in my room and slept most of the day. I couldn't keep my weight up and my energy had hit the floor. But every week we received constant comfort and encouragement from our sons and the rest of the family, which helped tremendously. It didn't occur to me until a few months later how difficult it must have been for them to see what their parents were going through. We were all going through this situation as a family.

Things began to change the more I learned about God's promises and applied them in my walk. I did not have to worry any longer. I did not have to fight this thing on my own or submit to it. We no longer had to walk under the death sentence of this disease. I accepted the fact that my life is not my own, it is my Lord's. My life is in the hands of my Lord God. Psalm 31:15 reminds us, "My times are in Your hand; Deliver me from the hand of my enemies," and Psalm 25:1-2 says, "To You, O Lord, I lift up my soul. O my God, I trust in You; Let me not be ashamed; Let not my enemies triumph over me."

When you hand your sickness over to God, you will begin to see your situation in a different light. You will see the things that were overtaking you start to go away. God becomes greater than your situation when you let Him. Worrying will be a choice and not a constant state of mind. Fear will be a choice that can be defeated with faith. The fear of not knowing what will happen tomorrow won't matter because our Lord God knows the outcome from the beginning. Doubt will be a choice that you can replace when you trust in the Lord. Don't wear yourself out worrying about things you have no control over.

I Trust You, Lord God

There will be days when you don't understand everything that is happening and begin to ask why your heart is heavy and your healing is taking forever. You'll question whether you will be healed at all or passed over. You'll have doubts about whether you're believing or doing enough with the Lord for your healing.

It's okay to have questions and to be real with God, but then quickly give thanks and declare that no matter what happens in your life, you will trust in Him, because He is able and faithful to save you. As your situation seems hopeless and you grapple with doubts and questions, know that the word of the Lord is your ultimate weapon and He will defend and deliver you.

Believe that God will get you to where you are supposed to be. Proverbs 3:5 says, "Trust in the Lord with all your heart, and lean not on your own understanding; In all your ways acknowledge Him, And He shall direct your paths." Nothing is random, for God is strategic. As you walk through your dark valley and encounter others who let you down, don't be shaken, continue believing in God.

Keep doing the right thing even when you don't understand. Isaiah 54:10 reminds us, "'For the mountains shall depart And the hills be removed, But My kindness shall not depart from you, Nor shall My covenant of peace be removed,' Says the Lord, who has mercy on you." God's mercies apply to you and your family, too.

My Heart Shall Rejoice in Your Salvation

Rejoice! Oh, rejoice my brothers and sisters in our Lord Christ! For the Lord has heard your cries and seen your tears and is fully aware of your situation! Make the scripture Psalm 61:1-4 a personal declaration that you will trust in God and in His assurances for you. Then write them on the tablet of your heart.

> The Lord has heard my cry; and attends to my prayer. When I cry from the end of the earth, and when my heart is overwhelmed; The Lord will lead me to the rock that is higher than all. For the Lord has been my shelter, a strong tower from my enemy. I will abide in My Lord's tabernacle forever; and trust in the shelter of His wings. Selah

When we trust in Him, our heart rejoices! Psalm 13:5 says, "But I have trusted in Your mercy; My heart shall rejoice in Your salvation." God is the rock of our salvation! Know that in your sickness, His power is revealed through you and perfected in you, so rejoice! Second Corinthians 12:9 says, "But he said to me, 'My grace is sufficient for you, for my power is made perfect in weakness'. Therefore I will boast all the more gladly about my weaknesses, so that Christ's power may rest on me" (NIV).

Although you may be suffering, feeling the weakest you've ever felt, betrayed by someone close to you, feeling lonely and like nobody understands, thinking you are worthless, incapable of being loved or loving someone else, God loves you! His love for you is everlasting and unfailing! His mercies cover all of you! Take comfort in knowing that when you are weak, then you will be strong, for Christ lives in you.

If you are going to walk in sickness for a season, why not do it with the joy of the Lord shining through you. Let those around you in your home, in your workplace, in the hospital, see Jesus living in and through you and the strength of the Lord at work in your life. Be ready to be used by God to witness to others or plant the seed by your testimony and be prepared to give an answer to all those who ask for the hope in you. (See 1 Peter 3:15.) You are being validated and the victory has already been won. Receive it in the name of Jesus, Amen.

Though you may not see it at the time, know God is working the situation for your good. Romans 8:28 reminds us, "And we know that all things work together for good to those who love God, to those who are called according to His purpose."

Blessed to Abound in Every Good Work

Be blessed more and more my brothers and sisters in Christ! The Lord has known you since you were in your mother's womb. (See Jeremiah 1:5.) He has made you and will take care of you! He has carried you since you were born and will continue to carry you throughout your life.

Isaiah 46:3-4 tells us, "Listen to Me, O house of Jacob, and all the remnant of the house of Israel, Who have been upheld by Me from birth, Who have been carried from the womb: Even to your old age, I am He, And even to gray hairs I will carry you! I have made, and I will bear; Even I will carry, and will deliver you." God's word was—and still is—a life-transforming word for me. His promises gave me hope during a dark season of my life when I could not see a future or purpose. When I became receptive to His word, I began to learn that God's promises applied to me as well. Even if I had faith the size of a mustard seed, I could still be a receiver of God's multitude of blessings. (See Matthew 17:20.) He wanted me not only to receive His blessings, but to trust and delight in Him, the author and finisher of my faith! (See Hebrews 12:2.)

Psalm 37:3-5 says, "Trust in the Lord, and do good; Dwell in the land, and feed on His faithfulness. Delight yourself also in the Lord, And He shall give you the desires of your heart. Commit your way to the Lord, trust also in Him, And He shall bring it to pass." I am ready to receive heaven's dew and earth's richness from our Lord God.

The God Who created me reminds me that every good and perfect gift is from above, and He promised to supply all my needs, according to the riches of his glory in Christ Jesus. (See James 1:17 and Philippians 4:19.) His provision is not limited by the state of our economy or the condition of the stock market. He encourages me not to doubt, not to be discouraged, and not to fear, for He is my God and refreshes my soul. He is good and worthy to be praised! He is full of mercy and grace and will strengthen and help me!

God is able to bless us beyond what we can think or ask. Second Corinthians 9:8 says "And God is able to bless you abundantly, so that in all things at all times, having all that you need, you will abound in every good work" (NIV).

The next time you receive bad news, remember God is good all the time! He's able to bless you, keep you, and give you peace in the midst of your situation. Though it may not be easy for you to trust Him at first, and though you may weep night after night, your joy comes in the morning. (See Psalm 30:5.) Jeremiah 17:7-8 reminds us:

Blessed is the man who trusts in the Lord, and whose hope is the Lord. For he shall be like a tree planted by the waters, which spreads out its roots by the river, and will not fear when heat comes; but its leaf will be green, and will not be anxious in the year of drought, nor will cease from yielding fruit.

My Covenant with God is Superior

My covenant relationship with God, which is mediated by my Lord and Savior, Jesus Christ, is superior to any other covenant formed before it. Whatever I was bound to before, I declare I'm no longer bound to it now, and it must depart from me, as it is no longer legal or binding over me, in the name of Jesus, amen. My body is the Lord's and no longer under a spiritual attack.

When the doctors can't figure out the root cause of a condition, I can be still and know that God is with me, and He is over those who are over me. I am my Heavenly Father's and proclaim this body, His temple, separated for God's Holy Spirit to dwell within. I now have access to my Heavenly Father through Christ Jesus, who intercedes for me. (See Romans 8:34.)

John 3:16 reminds me, "For God so loved the world that He gave His only begotten Son, that whoever believes in Him should not perish but have everlasting life." There is power in the name and blood of Jesus, all we must do is repent of our sins and place faith, turn from our old ways, believe in Him, be obedient to God, and invite Him into our hearts. He wants to be Lord over our lives.

Some of us make the decision to accept Christ a difficult one because of our past hurts, disappointments, self-reliance, intellect, pride, hypocrisy in the church, or being raised in a false religion. But, when we finally make the decision to take a step forward with Christ, we are forgiven, and our debt is paid once and for all! First Peter 2:24 says, "'He himself bore our sins' in his body on the cross, so that we might die to sins and live for righteousness; 'by his wounds you have been healed.'"

Christ laid His body down for all of mankind. Matthew 26:28 reminds us, "This is my blood of the covenant, which is poured out for many for the forgiveness of sins" (NIV). He not only laid His body down, but He raised it up again on the third day, and now sits at the right hand of God the Father, interceding on our behalf. For we have all sinned and fallen short of God's glory, but by His grace we have been saved through faith. (See Romans 3:23 and Ephesians 2:8.) He has given us a new gift, a new promise, a new life, a new future, and a new hope, if we have faith and believe in God.

John 6:53 reminds us, "Jesus said to them, 'Very truly I tell you, unless you eat the flesh of the Son of Man and drink his blood, you have no life in you.'" We are reminded that Jesus was 100-percent man and 100-percent God. He became flesh among us and poured out His blood for our sins. He is the Bread of Life and the well of living water, able to quench our thirst.

There is None Like Thee

God is great! We serve a mighty and everlasting God! He promises to renew our strength when we wait upon Him. (See Isaiah 40:31.) He is steadfast and does not grow weary or faint or powerless! His mighty power is at work within us. (See Ephesians 3:20.) All things are possible with God! (See Matthew 19:26.) What an assurance it is to know regardless of the situation and against all odds; when medical treatments and medicine fails; when doctors have given up and sent you home; there is still a mighty God Who can do the impossible!

He is a merciful God Who can heal you and your family emotionally, spiritually, and physically above what you can ever hope or ask for. Jeremiah 32:27 says, "Behold, I am the Lord, the God of all flesh. Is there anything too hard for Me?" All power belongs to Him and there is none like Him in Heaven or on earth!

Who would not be fearful of our Lord God's greatness? Jeremiah 10:6-7 tells us, "Inasmuch as there is none like You, O Lord (You are great, and Your name is great in might), Who would not fear You, O King of the nations? For this is Your rightful due. For among all the wise men of the nations, and in all their kingdoms, there is none like You."

Feeling lost? He will save you! Feeling unworthy of love? He will quiet you with His love! Feeling sad? He will give you gladness! Feeling alone? He is with you! Zephaniah 3:17 reminds us, "The Lord your God in your midst, The Mighty One, will save; He will rejoice over you with gladness, He will quiet you with His love, He will rejoice over you with singing." Sing to the Lord for He has been good to you! When you realize there are no guarantees in life other than God's word, who He is, and what He does, putting your trust in anything else is a risk with unfavorable and everlasting consequences. There is none like Him!

The Lord is Dealing Bountifully With Me

He didn't have to deliver me when I was living in darkness, but He did! The Lord has been good to me. He didn't have to offer a path to salvation when I was living in sin, but He did through His Son, Jesus! The Lord has been good to me. He didn't have to offer me rest when my soul was restless, but He did! The Lord has been good to me. He didn't have to give me faith when fear got a grip on me, but He did! The Lord has been good to me. He didn't have to comfort me in all my cares, but He did! The Lord has been good to me. He didn't have to give me peace when I pleaded for mercy, but He did! The Lord has been good to me. He didn't have to give me victory to overcome the world with our faith in the name of Jesus, but He did! The Lord is good to me.

Trust in the Lord for He is faithful and His plans for us are for good. Psalm 37:3-5 says, "Trust in the Lord, and do good; Dwell in the land, and feed on His faithfulness. Delight yourself also in the Lord, And He shall give you the desires of your heart. Commit your way to the Lord, trust also in Him, And He shall bring it to pass." Our God is a God of abundance.

Philippians 1-6 says,

Being confident of this very thing, that He who has begun a good work in you will complete it until the day of Jesus Christ.

He has abundantly blessed us and we abound in every good work because the Lord is good and faithful. He has given us everything we need to pursue and abound in every good work for His kingdom. Bless His name and be cheerful as you bring your tithes and offerings to His storehouse and acknowledge He is your provider and also the God of the bountiful harvest.

Mercies Over Me

God is a merciful God. He has changed the trajectory of my life. He has forgiven me of my sins. He shows mercy to me. I am covered by the love of a living and compassionate God. I have been created to fellowship with God. I exist to worship and glorify His name. He is mighty in power, and the Creator of the ends of the earth.

As I draw close to Him, He promises to draw close to me. (See James 4:8.) His mercy is at work within me. He has given me a measure of faith, a fresh beginning, a new future, a higher hope, and a new ministry. You can have this too. God is with us and in us so that others can see His great love and mercies at work through us. The Lord does great things and He is good to all! We are no longer living under the old law and wrath but under His mercy and grace. He gives grace to those who humble themselves. We have been redeemed by our Lord Jesus Christ! We are now the righteousness of God, in Christ. (See 2 Corinthians 5:21.) We no longer are to live in the dark but in the light.

My Breakthrough Draws Near

It is understandable when one is diagnosed with a sickness to immediately want to seek medical attention, or if a believer, to want to be instantly healed. If the healing is not immediate for any reason, we begin to question our faith, or even worse, we question whether or not God hears us or can deliver us. If we are not careful, we will lose our trust in God. There is no doubt God still performs miracles and does the impossible. We are reminded in the book of Hebrews, chapter 13, verse 8, "Jesus Christ is the same yesterday and today and forever." We sometimes forget He can make a way when it seems there can be no way. I started in search of physical healing instead of seeking a breakthrough for my spiritual condition. Isaiah 43:19 says, "Behold, I will do a new thing, Now it shall spring forth; Shall you not know it? I will even make a road in the wilderness And rivers in the desert." Did you catch it?

It's never a question of whether God can do it, He can deliver you! He is the God of creation, of all flesh, and of the ends of the earth! There's nothing impossible for Him! No one can challenge His authority, word, or plans. He not only created you and loves you with an everlasting love, but He is also working a new thing in you, if you let Him. His word produces results. It's impossible for God's word to return void. (See Isaiah 55:11.) Imagine what the new you would look like, if instead of focusing on your sickness, you actually began to plead with God for His compassion and mercy to heal all of you. Continually seeking Him to reveal His plan for you; to reveal Himself more to you; to heal you spiritually, emotionally, relationally, and physically; to use you to accomplish His will for you.

Oh friend, how you would begin to see things in a whole new light; how you will realize things about God through His word that would take on a new level of meaning and understanding; and how you would know that God is who He says He is and is with you in your valley. Take hold of His promises for you, and don't let Him pass by.

One of my spiritual breakthroughs came to me the night before a medical procedure that was going to have me sedated for up to 4 hours. I was told to view the act of laying on the table as an act of worship to God. That was a breakthrough for me! For years, I hated any type of medicine, medical treatment, and even the thought of being put to sleep by a sedative drug. In one second, the phrase "act of worship" put the attention back on God and it helped me. I could trust God that doctors are one of His tools to heal me using modern technology. Even more important was the fact that by surrendering myself to God, I no longer had to worry about the outcome. The assurance that God was over all the doctors who were over me; that He has the final say over my life; and His will would be done, made all the difference going in the next morning.

Jesus Always Rises

John 10:18 says, "No one takes it from Me, but I lay it down of Myself. I have power to lay it down, and I have power to take it again. This command I have received from My Father." Jesus humbled Himself and voluntarily laid down His life unto death on the cross for our sins. He could have prayed to God the Father and called upon more than twelve legions of angels available at His disposal, but instead He chose to be obedient to God and go to the cross for you and me. Matthew 26:53 says, "Or do you think that I cannot now pray to My Father, and He will provide Me with more than twelve legions of angels?"

Over twelve legions of angels are a massive number of angels and power! That is at least 72,000 angels awaiting the call to rain down supernatural and overwhelming power upon the soldiers who were holding Him like the world has not seen before—not even today. With each angel capable of wiping out 185,000 men, there was simply no match in response from the soldiers that would be able to withstand the onslaught coming, had Jesus not taken up His cup, shed His blood, and laid His life on the cross at Calvary. Jesus not only laid down His life, but He raised it up again. He arose again on the third day and lives! He is coming back, this time as a mighty warrior with a rod of iron and the armies of heaven, which no one knows the time or day when He will return. (See Matthew 24:36.)

Revelation 19:13-16 says,

> He was clothed with a robe dipped in blood, and His name is called The Word of God. And the armies in heaven, clothed in fine linen, white and clean, followed Him on white horses. Now out of His mouth goes a sharp sword, that with it He should strike the nations. And He Himself will rule them with a rod of iron. He Himself treads the winepress of the fierceness and wrath of Almighty God. And He has on His robe and on His thigh a name written:
>
> KING OF KINGS AND
> LORD OF LORDS.

I don't know about you, but the sheer amount of power available in heaven reminds me of how there is no lack with God. How He is the God of abundance! Deuteronomy 28:12 says, "The Lord will open to you His good treasure, the heavens, to give the rain to your land in its season, and to bless all the work of your hand. You shall lend to many nations, but you shall not borrow."

Share Your Testimony

One time I had just been prayed over at Casa Paternal church and it was revealed to me that I needed to let go of all unforgiveness. The very next day I had a medical procedure and as I waited in bed, I felt the need to share my experience with a nurse by my side. To my surprise, she told me she was struggling with unforgiveness. Her neighbor had said something to her that had upset her. I urged her to forgive her neighbor and let go of unforgiveness right away.

I shared with her that forgiveness is more for her than for her neighbor—it releases her from resentment and anger that can fester over time and block God's forgiveness and blessings for her. We are forgiven that we may also forgive others. I went on to tell her how as the people had laid hands on me recently, I felt an intense heat on my head and was overcome emotionally.

Just as I was speaking, she turned to me weeping and said, "I feel the heat you are describing." Moments later she got an instant message alert and it was her neighbor! She was stunned, to say the least, at the timing of it all. After the procedure was done, she had to call for an IV and to reserve a room for me. Her very next words were, "This is freaky." I asked her if everything was okay and she said a special friend of hers who was more of a mother figure to her had just passed away just a few days before on the 22nd of the month, and the room they had assigned for me was room number 22.

Honestly, I didn't know what to make of it at first, I thought, *This can't be good for me*. But glory be to God, the nurse felt and witnessed something unusual that morning. She wasn't even scheduled to work on that day. My faith was increased as I witnessed a glimpse of how sharing my testimony made a difference in her day. She gave more thought to forgiveness on that Friday than she had probably planned to. I believe she was touched by the Holy Spirit.

You would be surprised how many people need a testimony from another person who has gone through it. A need for a word of encouragement, a compassionate listener, or simply a hug. God designed us to love and fellowship with Him and with each other. We all need each other. We all need prayer and to pray for one another. When we go astray from loving God with all our heart, soul, and mind, and loving our neighbor as ourselves, we become isolated, distant, and untrusting. This opens many doors for the devil to gain legal access into our lives. Pride creeps up and attempts to promote itself above God and builds a superiority complex in the opposite direction of love.

It's easy to reason our way out of doing the right thing for others and pour ourselves into our profession or work. Eventually, our way will lead us to form habits that will one day overtake us and bring us to the end of ourselves. The dismissal of love is subtle and stems from being insulted, let down, abused, or rejected. Another thing that can taint our love for God, others, and ourselves is a religious system, a false understanding of God's word, or being betrayed by other believers or the church. If you are not careful, your love will grow cold. Your thirst for lasting fulfilment will never be satisfied outside of God's love for you. There is no substitute for His love.

If you haven't attended an encounter retreat through your church, I strongly recommend you sign up and go to one. Don't wait for years to go by before you go, like some do in the church. Jump at the opportunity to get away for a couple of days to draw close to God. The key thing to remember is that as much as you are willing to peel back the layers of the onion of your life before God, is as much as God will show up. While those who attend take a vow not to disclose what happens at encounter, when I say that it is life changing, it's all that and more. You really don't know what to expect, except you will encounter God before the weekend is over.

While it's great to share your testimony with others, it's equally beneficial when you are on the receiving end and others speak a word of knowledge into your life. This is exactly what happened to me. On three separate occasions by three different people, over a period of about three months, I received confirmation that God's healing of my end-stage disease would be used as a ministry to help others and bring glory to God. I would be healed to help heal others. It's not by my works but by the grace of God and His mercy that this is all possible in the mighty name of Jesus Christ, Amen.

This book you are reading is an example of something I had no clue I would do. In fact, I was so deep in the swamp for over a year, that the last thing on my mind was to write a book about it. Who would want to relive through the most painful experience of one's life over and over again as required when writing a book? But writing a book kept coming up from members in my family, people I met in the medical field, and with my brothers and sisters at church. I was constantly told how my story would help so many people struggling with illness. How there are many lying in hospital beds right now without hope, comfort, or the truth of God's love and mercy for them.

I remember being called back in to the hospital by an employee safety representative from where I had just been drained. One of the registered technicians was accidentally exposed to my ascites fluid and they needed to test me for a viral disease. As I sat there to have blood drawn, I shared with the representative my testimony of all that God had done for me through this situation. She was touched by the testimony. Just as I was getting ready to leave about twenty minutes later, she told me I should consider coming back to the hospital to share my testimony with the other patients. She said it would help many of them.

Another time I was in New Mexico getting IV treatment when an elderly woman, whom I had never met before, sat down to my right. A little while after, I felt led to share God's promise list with her, and tell her how it had helped me during my situation. She viewed the list on my phone and I text it to her. As I prepared to leave, I ran into her again, and this time she was with her husband. I asked them if it was okay to pray for them.

To my surprise, they said yes, and little did I know then that they were going through a very tough time. We all wept. One of the nurses from the clinic noticed us outside. I also had a chance to share my testimony with her, and to this day we remain friends. To God be all the glory! You never know when your testimony will touch someone and make a difference.

Lessons Learned

The unexpected news of being diagnosed with a life-threatening stage-4 disease is enough to overwhelm anyone. It's a constant reminder of the clear and present danger we live in—the devil is trying to steal the word of God in you, kill the body of Christ (the church), and destroy our testimony for Jesus. In the natural, it may seem like a strictly physical matter, but there is a spiritual element that requires studying the word of God. Many of us are quick to take the medicine and not the manna from heaven. Last time I checked there is no medicine that can take away the sin of the world, only the blood of Christ can do that. The bread of life is still able to perform the miraculous. It's important to remember that.

Inform your pastor, church elders, and family of believers, of your medical situation and start a circle of family prayer support. Don't go it alone! If you don't belong to a church, find a local bible-based church and start attending services. Get involved at church and don't be afraid to share your need for prayer for healing. Introduce yourself to the pastor and ask him or her to pray over you. Ask the elders of the church to pray for you as well. (See James 5:14.) As often as possible, when an altar call is announced, be the first to the altar for prayer. Schedule a meeting with your pastor and share your struggles. If the church offers a healing class, sign up for it, show up, and participate.

Make it a point to surround yourself with as many like-minded Christians as possible and build your circle of believers. Attend any seminars offered by the church to build your faith and go to events to fellowship with other believers. There is no greater feeling next to knowing that God loves you and is with you, than of knowing there are believers ready to stand in the gap for you and help carry your burdens. Having a family who also prays is a tremendous help. My wife and sons were so incredible in walking through this valley with me and encouraging me. Their love and words of encouragement also kept me going. My daughter-and-law kept reminding me I was a warrior of God. I appreciate all the prayers from everyone and the shed tears I never saw but God knows who you are.

Stay positive! Remember that God is faithful even unto Himself and His word. His word will not return void. What He says will come to pass. Having that assurance, throw away any and all negative thoughts along with the victim mentality, the spirit of self-pity, that normally strikes a person upon learning of a disease or a disaster. Trust in God for your victory and let Him defend you. He promises to fight for you when you put your trust in Him and give Him a chance.

You will have good days and some challenging days. When you feel negative thoughts or fear coming on, take the attention off yourself and focus on God for Who He is and what He does for you! Begin to thank God that He has sown great seeds in you. Thank God that He is the same yesterday, today, and forever. Thank God that His plan for you is to prosper you and not harm you. Thank God that He wants to give you a future and a hope unlike the world can give. Go to the chapter on God's promise list and begin to speak out loud the promises heading your way. His blessings will track you down and tackle you. Keep in mind the more pressure you feel, and the more desperate things get, the closer you are to victory. He will give you victory.

Be in His Word! When you spend time in His Word you are spending one-on-one time with Jesus! Seek Him early in the morning. Give Him the first fruits of each day.

Speak with your doctor and find out if you can exercise, based upon your medical condition. At a minimum, see if you can walk daily. Once I got the green light from my doctor, I started walking. Create a playlist based on Christian and uplifting music and pray as you walk. I gradually started working out 20 minutes each on a stairmaster, elliptical, or treadmill and then slowly introduced lifting weights. Meditate on God's promises as you exercise. Use the promise list and playlist when you are in the waiting room preparing for your next appointment or procedure. Get prayed up and stay upbeat. Take what is available to you based on your level of faith but put your trust in God for your healing.

Don't wait for the perfect time to submit yourself to God. Turn to Him now and acknowledge Him in all your ways. As you prepare for your next procedure, offer your body as an act of worship to God. Tell God that you trust in Him and give Him honor, glory, and praise. Prepare your heart and ask the Holy Spirit if He has a word of knowledge for someone you are about to meet in your next procedure. I was able to share my testimony of God's faithfulness with the nurses and technicians while I was still in the valley laying on the bed. Let them see the joy of Jesus flow through you. Don't worry about your circumstances, surrender them to God. When you think about it, Jesus purchased all of you, so your sins and situations are no longer yours. You have been paid for! Surrender them all to Him! When you stumble and sin, repent and place your faith in the Father. Remember, the more difficult the valley gets or the bigger the giant appears, the more your victory is at hand in the name of Jesus, Amen.

Proverbs 3:5-9 reminds us to,

> Trust in the Lord with all your heart, and lean not on your own understanding; In all your ways acknowledge Him, and He shall direct your paths. Do not be wise in your own eyes; Fear the Lord and depart from evil. It will be health to your flesh, and strength to your bones. Honor the Lord with your possessions, and with the first fruits of all your increase.

As you face your giants in life, know that there is no situation too enormous for God to handle. You and your situation matter to God. He's into the details of your life. Grab hold of His garment as He passes you by. His angels encamp around you. Be surrounded by the word of God and followers of Christ. Experience God's forgiveness, mercy, grace, and supernatural healing for you and your family. May His presence and power become so real for you it completely overwhelms you the more you trust in Him. Allow Him to work out His plan in and through you. As He unveils His perfect will for you, may you serve Him and commit to blessing others as you are blessed. Don't engage in self-pity. God will provide a way out for you in His time and His way. Don't just settle for a physical healing but avail yourself to His emotional healing, spiritual healing, relational healing, financial healing, and healing your faith, while you wait for your physical healing. For the God who calls you is faithful! He also will do it! See your victory! Claim your victory! Speak your victory! Walk in His victory against all odds and in the name above every other name, our Lord and Savior, Jesus Christ, Amen!

CPSIA information can be obtained
at www.ICGtesting.com
Printed in the USA
LVHW040155191219
641008LV00003B/35/P